Friendship

Friendship

HUGH BLACK

www.joshuapress.com

Co-published by
Joshua Press Inc., Guelph, Ontario, Canada
Leith Books, Fenstanton, England

Distributed by
Sola Scriptura Ministries International
www.sola-scriptura.ca

Originally published in 1898
First Joshua Press edition 2008

Book and cover design © 2008 Janice Van Eck
Typeset in Bickham Script Pro and 11/14.5 pt Bembo

Library and Archives Canada Cataloguing in Publication
Black, Hugh, 1868-1953
Friendship / Hugh Black.

ISBN 978-1-894400-28-2 (BOUND)
ISBN 978-1-894400-27-5 (PAPERBACK)

1. Friendship. I. Title.
BJ1533.F8B53 2008   177'.62   C2008-900473-6

To friends—who make our lives rich

Contents

Entreat me not to leave thee,
And to return from following after thee:
For whither thou goest, I will go;
And where thou lodgest, I will lodge:
Thy people shall be my people,
And thy God my God:
Where thou diest, will I die,
And there will I be buried:
The Lord do so to me, and more also,
If aught but death part thee and me.

~ RUTH 1:16-17

Preface

This edition of Hugh Black's *Friendship* (1898) is the result of the efforts of two friends who so enjoyed discovering this title and appreciated the value of it in their lives. Both have been blessed with the gift of friendship—with God, with one another and with others who have enriched our lives with their presence and counsel. We hope that many readers will find this title helpful as they seek to find and build healthy, lasting friendships.

Every book, whether a reprint of a classic or a new work, involves the collaboration of others. For this reprint, we are indebted to those of our friends who have contributed towards its publication. In addition, we are thankful for Pamela Bugden who assisted us in inputting the text and Karen Van Zanden who proofread the final copy.

With thankfulness to God, we dedicate this book to our friends—thank you for making our lives rich!

~ HILARY BUGDEN, *Fenstanton, England*
   & JANICE VAN ECK, *Guelph, Ontario, Canada*

Friendship is to be valued for what there is in it, not for what can be gotten out of it. When two people appreciate each other because each has found the other convenient to have around, they are not friends, they are simply acquaintances with a business understanding. To seek friendship for its utility is as futile as to seek the end of a rainbow for its bag of gold. A true friend is always useful in the highest sense; but we should beware of thinking of our friends as brother members of a mutual-benefit association with its periodical demands and threats of suspension for non-payment of dues.

~ HENRY CLAY TRUMBULL

Introduction

by Michael A.G. Haykin

Our culture in the past hundred years has not been one that has provided great encouragement for the nurture and development of deep, long-lasting, satisfying friendships. Such friendships take time and sacrifice, and in the twentieth century, the culture that came to rule in the west was a busy world that was far more interested in receiving and possessing than sacrificing and giving.[1]

What is especially disturbing about this fact is that twentieth-century western Christianity was little different from its culture.

---

1 See Diogenes Allen, *Love: Christian Romance, Marriage, Friendship* (Cambridge, Massachusetts: Cowley Publications, 1987), 45-46.

Friendship

The English Anglican writer C. S. Lewis has an ingenious little book entitled *The Screwtape Letters*, a remarkable commentary on spiritual warfare from the point of view of our Enemy. In it there is one letter from the senior devil, Screwtape, to his nephew Wormwood in which Screwtape rejoices over the fact that "in modern Christian writings" there is to be found "few of the old warnings about Worldly Vanities, the Choice of Friends, and the Value of Time."[2] Now, whether or not Lewis is right with regard to a scarcity of twentieth-century Christian literature about "Worldly Vanities" and "the Value of Time," he is undoubtedly correct when it comes to the topic of friendship.

Now, before Lewis had noted this trend, the Scottish theologian Hugh Black (1868-1953) had analyzed it in this gem of a book and sought to provide a remedy. Black was a Scottish pastor and writer who emigrated to the United States at the beginning of the twentieth century, where he became a relatively well-known speaker on homiletics. Black ably shows how different in this respect is the world of the modern west from that of the ancients, both pagan and Christian. In the ancient world friendship was deemed to be of such vital importance that the pagan philosopher Plato devoted an entire book, the *Lysis*, as well as substantial portions of two other books, the *Phaedrus* and the *Symposium*, to a treatment of its nature. Aristotle, the other leading thinker of the classical Greek period, also considered the topic of friendship significant enough to have a discussion of it occupy two of the ten books of the *Nicomachean Ethics*, his major work on ethical issues. For the ancient Greeks—and this is true also of the Romans—friendship formed one of the highest ideals of human life.

Although we do not find such extended discussions of the concept of friendship in the Scriptures, we do come across reflections on friendship like Ecclesiastes 4:7-12 and marvellous illustrations of

---

2 *The Screwtape Letters,* Letter 10 in *The Best of C. S. Lewis* (Washington, D.C.: Canon Press, 1969), 43.

what friendship should be like, for example, that of Ruth and Naomi, David and Jonathan, and Jesus and his disciples. In John 15:15 Jesus says, "No longer do I call you servants, for the servant does not know what his master is doing; but I have called you friends, for all that I have heard from my Father I have made known to you," showing that believers enjoy that wonderful relationship with him as well. And then there are nuggets of advice about having friends and keeping them in that Old Testament compendium of wisdom, Proverbs, which Black calls "a treatise on friendship."[3] These texts leave the impression that the world of the Bible regards friendship as a very important part of life. Now, the Bible uses two central images in its representation of friendship.[4]

The first is that friendship involves the *knitting together of souls*. Deuteronomy provides the earliest mention of this, when it describes "a friend who is as your own soul" (Deuteronomy 13:6), that is, a friend is a companion of one's innermost thoughts and feelings.[5] This is well illustrated by Jonathan and David's friendship, described for us in 1 Samuel 18:1-4. Here we see that the privileges and responsibilities of a biblical friend entail strong emotional attachment and loyalty.[6]

The second image that the Bible uses to represent friendship is *the face-to-face encounter*. This is literally the image used for Moses' relationship to God: in the tabernacle God spoke to Moses "face to face, as a man speaks to his friend" (Exodus 33:11; Numbers 12:8). The image of a face-to-face encounter implies conversation, a sharing of confidences and consequently a meeting of minds, goals and direction. One of the benefits of such face-to-face encounters between friends is the heightened insight that such encounters produce. A proverb that highlights this idea is the famous one in Proverbs 27:17: "Iron sharpens iron, and one friend sharpens another."

---

3 See page 19.

4 "Friendship," *Dictionary of Biblical Imagery*, eds. Leland Ryken *et al.* (Downers Grove, Illinois/Leicester: InterVarsity Press, 1998), 308-309.

5 See pages 27, 37-38, 54.

6 See pages 10-13, 26, 41.

It is instructive to observe that the spread of the church throughout the Roman Empire in the centuries immediately after the death
and resurrection of Christ did not negate this rich appreciation of
friendship. Despite the Christian emphasis on showing love to all
men and women—family, friends, acquaintances, even enemies—
friendship continued to be highly valued. In fact, the emphasis placed
on the unity in Christ of all Christians encouraged a high degree of
spiritual intimacy that resembled, and even surpassed, the intimacy
considered by Graeco-Roman paganism to be essential to the experience of genuine friendship.[7]

Gregory of Nazianzus (c.329-389), a leading fourth-century Greek
Christian theologian, could thus write of his friendship with Basil
of Caesarea (c.330-379) during their time together as students in
Athens in the 350s: "In studies, in lodgings, in discussions I had him
as companion….We had all things in common….But above all it
was God, of course, and a mutual desire for higher things, that drew
us to each other. As a result we reached such a pitch of confidence
that we revealed the depths of our hearts, becoming ever more united
in our yearning."[8] Given this estimation of friendship, it is no surprise
that Gregory could also state: "If anyone were to ask me, 'What is
the best thing in life?' I would answer, 'Friends.'"[9]

This little book on friendship will help to recapture these classical
perspectives on friendship. Black not only discusses the nature of
friendship, but he provides advice on how to choose friends and
when one has them, how to keep them. In harmony with his
Reformed heritage, Black is conscious of the limits of human
friendship—it is no substitute for friendship with God. Black would
have agreed with the eighteenth-century Anglican rector James

7 Carolinne White, *Christian Friendship in the Fourth Century* (Cambridge:
Cambridge University Press, 1992), 57.

8 *De vita sua* 225ff. [trans. Denise Molaise Meehan, *Saint Gregory of Nazianzus:
Three Poems* (*The Fathers of the Church*, vol. 75; Washington, D.C.: The Catholic
University of America Press, 1987), 83-84].

9 Cited White, *Christian Friendship*, 70.

Newton, who, when faced with the death of his brother, wrote: "If we have God for our Friend, what need we to fear? Nothing. But without his Friendship we may be looked on as the most miserable of Men."

~ MICHAEL A.G. HAYKIN
   Professor of Biblical Spirituality and Church History
   Southern Baptist Theological Seminary, Louisville, Kentucky

But, far away from these, another sort
Of lovers linkëd in true heart's consent;
Which lovëd not as these for like intent,
But on chaste virtue grounded their desire,
Far from all fraud or feignëd blandishment;
Which, in their spirits kindling zealous fire,
Brave thoughts and noble deeds did evermore aspire.

Such were great Hercules and Hylas dear;
True Jonathan and David trusty tried;
Stout Theseus and Pirithöys his fere;
Pylades and Orestes by his side;
Mild Titus and Gesippus without pride;
Damon and Pythias, whom death could not sever;
All these, and all that ever had been tied
In bands of friendship, there did live forever;
Whose lives although decay'd, yet loves decayëd never.
~ EDMUND SPENSER, *The Faerie Queene*

Chapter 1

The Miracle of Friendship

T he idea, so common in the ancient writers, is not all a
poetic conceit, that the soul of a man is only a fragment
of a larger whole, and goes out in search of other souls
in which it will find its true completion. We walk among
worlds unrealized, until we have learned the secret of love. We know
this, and in our sincerest moments admit this, even though we are
seeking to fill up our lives with other ambitions and other hopes.

Friendship

It is more than a dream of youth that there may be here a satisfaction of the heart, without which, and in comparison with which, all worldly success is failure. In spite of the selfishness which seems to blight all life, our hearts tell us that there is possible a nobler relationship of disinterestedness and devotion. Friendship in its accepted sense is not the highest of the different grades in that relationship, but it has its place in the kingdom of love, and through it we bring ourselves into training for a still larger love. The natural man may be self-absorbed and self-centred, but in a truer sense it is natural for him to give up self and link his life on to others. Hence the joy with which he makes the great discovery, that he is something to another and another is everything to him. It is the higher-natural for which he has hitherto existed. It is a miracle, but it happens.

The cynic may speak of the now obsolete sentiment of friendship, and he can find much to justify his cynicism. Indeed, on the first blush, if we look at the relative place the subject holds in ancient as compared to modern literature, we might say that friendship is a sentiment that is rapidly becoming obsolete. In pagan writers friendship takes a much larger place than it now receives. The subject bulks largely in the works of Plato, Aristotle, Epictetus, Cicero. And among modern writers it gets most importance in the writings of the more pagan-spirited, such as Montaigne. In all the ancients systems of philosophy, friendship was treated as an integral part of the system. To the Stoic it was a blessed occasion for the display of nobility and the native virtues of the human mind. To the Epicurean it was the most refined of the pleasures which made life worth living. In the *Nicomachean Ethics*, Aristotle makes it the culminating point, and out of the ten books gives two to the discussion of friendship. He makes it even the link of connection between his treatise on ethics and his companion treatise on politics. It is to him both the perfection of the individual life, and the bond that holds states together. Friendship is not only a beautiful and noble thing for a man, but the realization of it is also the ideal for the state; for if the citizens be friends, then justice, which is the great concern of all organized societies, is more than secured. Friendship is thus made the flower of ethics, and the root of politics.

Plato also makes friendship the ideal of the state, where all have common interests and mutual confidence. And apart from its place of prominence in systems of thought, perhaps a finer list of beautiful sayings about friendship could be culled from ancient writers than from modern. Classical mythology also is full of instances of great friendship, which almost assumed the place of a religion itself.

It is not easy to explain why its part in Christian ethics is so small in comparison. The change is due to an enlarging of the thought and life of man. Modern ideals are wider and more impersonal, just as the modern conception of the state is wider. The Christian ideal of love even for enemies has swallowed up the narrower ideal of philosophic friendship. Then possibly also the instinct finds satisfaction elsewhere in the modern man. For example, marriage, in more cases than ever before, supplies the need of friendship. Men and women are nearer in intellectual pursuits and in common tastes than they have ever been, and can be in a truer sense companions. And the deepest explanation of all is that the heart of man receives a religious satisfaction impossible before. Spiritual communion makes a man less dependent on human intercourse. When the heaven is as brass and makes no sign, men are thrown back on themselves to eke out their small stores of love.

At the same time friendship is not an obsolete sentiment. It is as true now as in Aristotle's time that no one would care to live without friends, though he has all other good things. It is still necessary to our life in its largest sense. The danger of sneering at friendship is that it may be discarded or neglected, not in the interests of a more spiritual affection, but to minister to a debased cynical self-indulgence. There is possible today, as ever, a generous friendship which forgets self. The history of the heart-life of man proves this. What records we have of such in the literature of every country! Peradventure for a good man men have even dared to die. Mankind has been glorified by countless silent heroisms, by unselfish service, and sacrificing love.

Christ, who always took the highest ground in His estimate of men, and never once put man's capacity for the noble on a low level, made the high-water mark of human friendship the standard of His own great action, "Greater love hath no man than this, that a man lay down his life for his friends."[1] This high-water mark has often been reached. Men have given themselves to each other, with nothing to gain, with no self-interest to serve, and with no keeping back part of the price. It is false to history to base life on selfishness, to leave out the list of human motives the highest of all. The miracle of friendship has been too often enacted on this dull earth of ours, to suffer us to doubt either its possibility or its wondrous beauty.

The classic instance of David and Jonathan represents the typical friendship. They met, and at the meeting knew each other to be nearer than kindred. By subtle elective affinity they felt that they belonged to each other. Out of all the chaos of the time and the disorder of their lives, there arose for these two souls a new and beautiful world, where there reigned peace, and love, and sweet content. It was the miracle of the death of self. Jonathan forgot his pride, and David his ambition. It was the smile of God which changed the world to them. One of them it saved from the temptations of a squalid court, and the other from the sourness of an exile's life. Jonathan's princely soul had no room for envy and jealousy. David's frank nature rose to meet the magnanimity of his friend.

In the kingdom of love there was no disparity between the king's son and the shepherd boy. Such a gift as each gave and received is not to be bought and sold. It was the fruit of the innate nobility of both: it softened and tempered a very trying time for both. Jonathan withstood his father's anger to shield his friend; David was patient with Saul for his son's sake. They agreed to be true to each other in their difficult position. Close and tender must have been the bond, which has such fruit in princely generosity and mutual loyalty of soul. Fitting was the beautiful lament, when David's heart was bereaved

1 John 15:13

at tragic Gilboa, "I am distressed for thee, my brother Jonathan: very pleasant hast thou been unto me: thy love to me was wonderful, passing the love of women."[2] Love is always wonderful, a new creation, fair and fresh to every loving soul. It is the miracle of spring to a cold dull earth.

When Montaigne wrote his essay on friendship,[3] he could do little but tell the story of his friend. The essay continually reverts to this, with joy that he had been privileged to have such a friend, with sorrow at his loss. It is a chapter of his heart. There was an element of necessity about it, as there is about all the great things of life. He could not account for it. It came to him without effort or choice. It was a miracle, but it happened. "If a man should importune me to give a reason why I loved him, I can only answer, because it was he, because it was I." It was as some secret appointment of heaven. They were both grown men when they first met, and death separated them soon. "If I should compare all my life with the four years I had the happiness to enjoy the sweet society of this excellent man, it is nothing but smoke; an obscure and tedious night from the day that I lost him. I have led a sorrowful and languishing life ever since. I was so accustomed to be always his second in all places and in all interests, that methinks I am now no more than half a man, and have but half a being." We would hardly expect such passion of love and regret from the easy-going, genial, garrulous essayist.

The joy that comes from a true communion of heart with another is perhaps one of the purest and greatest in the world, but its function is not exhausted by merely giving pleasure. Though we may not be conscious of it, there is a deeper purpose in it, an education in the highest arts of living. We may be enticed by the pleasure it affords, but its greatest good is got by the way. Even intellectually it means the opening of a door into the mystery of life. Only love *understands* after all. It gives insight. We cannot truly know anything without

---

2 2 Samuel 1:26

3 Michel de Montaigne, *Of Friendship* (1580)

sympathy, without getting out of self and entering into others. A man cannot be a true naturalist, and observe the ways of birds and insects accurately, unless he can watch long and lovingly. We can never know children, unless we love them. Many of the chambers of the house of life are forever locked to us, until love gives us the key.

To learn to love all kinds of nobleness gives insights into the true significance of things, and gives a standard to settle their relative importance. An uninterested spectator sees nothing, or, what is worse, sees wrongly. Most of our mean estimates of human nature in modern literature, and our false realisms in art, and our stupid pessimisms in philosophy, are due to an unintelligent reading of surface facts. Men set out to note and collate impressions, and make perhaps a scientific study of slumdom, without genuine interest in the lives they see, and therefore without true insight into them. They miss the inwardness, which love alone can supply. If we look without love we can only see the outside, the mere form and expression of the subject studied. Only with tender compassion and loving sympathy can we see the beauty even in the eye dull with weeping and in the fixed face pale with care. We will often see noble patience shining through them, and loyalty to duty, and virtues and graces unsuspected by others.

The divine meaning of a true friendship is that it is often the first unveiling of the secret of love. It is not an end in itself, but has most of its worth in what it leads to, the priceless gift of seeing with the heart rather than with the eyes. To love one soul for its beauty and grace and truth is to open the way to appreciate all beautiful and true and gracious souls, and to recognize spiritual beauty wherever it is seen.

The possibility at least of friendship must be a faith with us. The cynical attitude is an offence. It is possible to find in the world true-hearted, leal[4] and faithful dealing between man and man. To doubt this is to doubt the divine in life. Faith in man is essential to faith in God. In spite of all deceptions and disillusionments, in spite of all

---

4 Scottish idiom meaning loyal and true.

the sham fellowships, in spite of the flagrant cases of self-interest and callous cruelty, we must keep clear and bright our faith in the possibilities of our nature. The man who hardens his heart because he has been imposed on has no real belief in virtue, and with suitable circumstances could become the deceiver instead of the deceived. The great miracle of friendship with its infinite wonder and beauty may be denied to us, and yet we may believe in it. To believe that it is possible is enough, even though in its superbest form it has never come to us. To possess it, is to have one of the world's sweetest gifts.

Aristotle defines friendship as one soul abiding in two bodies. There is no explaining such a relationship, but there is no denying it. It has not deserted the world since Aristotle's time. Some of our modern poets have sung of it with as brave a faith as ever poet of old. What splendid monuments to friendship we possess in Milton's *Lycidas* and Tennyson's *In Memoriam!* In both there is the recognition of the spiritual power of it, as well as the joy and comfort it brought. The grief is tempered by an awed wonder and a glad memory.

The finest feature of Rudyard Kipling's work, and it is a constant feature of it, is the comradeship between commonplace soldiers of no high moral or spiritual attainment, and yet it is the strongest force in their lives, and on occasion makes heroes of them. We feel that their faithfulness to each other is almost the only point at which their souls are reached. The threefold cord of his soldiers, vulgar in mind and common in thought as they are, is a cord which we feel is not easily broken, and it is their friendship and loyalty to each other which save them from utter vulgarity.

In Walt Whitman there is the same insight into the force of friendship in ordinary life, with added wonder at the miracle of it. He is the poet of comrades, and sings the song of companionship more than any other theme. He ever comes back to the lifelong love of comrades. The mystery and the beauty of it impressed him:

O tan-faced prairie-boy,
Before you came to camp came many a welcome gift,

Praises and presents came and nourishing food, till at last among the recruits

You came, taciturn, with nothing to give—we but looked on each other,

When lo! more than all the gifts of the world you gave me.[5]

After all, in spite of the vulgar materialism of our day, we do feel that the spiritual side of life is the most important, and brings the only true joy. And friendship in its essence is spiritual. It is the free, spontaneous outflow of the heart, and is a gift from the great Giver.

Friends are born, not made. At least it is so with the higher sort. The marriage of souls is a heavenly mystery, which we cannot explain, and which we need not try to explain. The method by which it is brought about differs very much, and depends largely on temperament. Some friendships grow and ripen slowly and steadily with the years. We cannot tell where they began, or how. They have become part of our lives, and we just accept them with sweet content and glad confidence. We have discovered that somehow we are rested, and inspired, by a certain companionship; that we understand and are understood easily.

Or it may come like love at first sight, by the thrill of elective affinity. This latter is the more uncertain, and needs to be tested and corrected by the trial of the years that follow. It has to be found out whether it is really spiritual kinship, or mere emotional impulse. It is a matter of temper and character. A naturally reserved person finds it hard to open his heart, even when his instinct prompts him; while a sociable, responsive nature is easily companionable. It is not always this quick attachment, however, which wears best, and that is the reason why youthful friendships have the character of being so fickle. They are due to a natural instinctive delight in society. Most young people find it easy to be agreeable, and are ready to place themselves under new influences.

But whatever the method by which a true friendship is formed,

---

5   Walt Whitman, *Leaves of Grass* (1867)

whether the growth of time or the birth of sudden sympathy, there seems, on looking back, to have been an element of necessity. It is a sort of predestined spiritual relationship. We speak of a man meeting his fate, and we speak truly. When we look back we see it to be like destiny; life converged to life, and there was no getting out of it even if we wished it. It is not that we made a choice, but that the choice made us. If it has come gradually, we waken to the presence of the force which has been in our lives, and has come into them never hasting but never resting, till now we know it to be an eternal possession. Or, as we are going about other business, never dreaming of the thing which occurs, the unexpected happens; on the road a light shines on us, and life is never the same again.

In one of its aspects, faith is the recognition of the inevitableness of providence; and when it is understood and accepted, it brings a great consoling power into the life. We feel that we are in the hands of a Love that orders our ways, and the knowledge means serenity and peace. The fatality of friendship is gratefully accepted, as the fatality of birth. To the faith which sees love in all creation, all life becomes harmony, and all sorts of loving relationships among men seem to be part of the natural order of the world. Indeed, such miracles are only to be looked for, and if absent from the life of man would make it hard to believe in the love of God.

The world thinks we idealize our friend, and tells us that love is proverbially blind. Not so: it is only love that sees, and thus can "win the secret of a weed's plain heart."[6] We only see what dull eyes never see at all. If we wonder what another man sees in his friend, it should be the wonder of humility, not the supercilious wonder of pride. He sees something which we are not permitted to witness. Beneath and amongst what looks only like worthless slag, there may glitter the pure gold of a fair character. That anybody in the world should be got to love us, and to see in us not what colder eyes see, not even what we are but what we may be, should of itself make us humble and

---

6 James Russell Lowell, *Sonnet XXV*

gentle in our criticism of others' friendships. Our friends see the best *in* us, and by that very fact call forth the best *from* us.

The great difficulty in this whole subject is that the relationship of friendship should so often be one-sided. It seems strange that there should be so much unrequited affection in the world. It seems almost impossible to get a completely balanced union. One gives so much more, and has to be content to get so much less. One of the most humiliating things in life is when another seems to offer his friendship lavishly, and we are unable to respond. So much love seems to go a-begging. So few attachments seem complete. So much affection seems unrequited.

But are we sure it is unrequited? The difficulty is caused by our common selfish standards. Most people, if they had their choice, would prefer to be loved rather than to love, if only one of the alternatives were permitted. That springs from the root of selfishness in human nature, which makes us think that possession brings happiness. But the glory of life is to love, not to be loved; to give, not to get; to serve, not to be served. It may not be our fault that we cannot respond to the offer of friendship or love, but it is our misfortune. The secret is revealed to the other, and hid from us. The gain is to the other, and the loss is to us. The miracle is the love, and to the lover comes the wonder of it, and the joy.

How were Friendship possible? In mutual devotedness to the
Good and True: otherwise impossible, except as Armed Neutrality,
or hollow Commercial League. A man, be the Heavens ever praised,
is sufficient for himself; yet were ten men, united in Love, capable of
being and of doing what ten thousand singly would fail in.
Infinite is the help man can yield to man.
~ THOMAS CARLYLE, *Sartor Resartus*

Chapter 2

The Culture of Friendship

The Book of Proverbs might almost be called a treatise on friendship, so full is it of advice about the sort of person a young man should consort with, and the sort of person he should avoid. It is full of shrewd, and prudent, and wise, sometimes almost worldly-wise, counsel. It is caustic in its satire about false friends, and about the way in which friendships are broken.

"The rich hath many friends,"[1] with an easily understood implication concerning their quality. "Every man is a friend to him that giveth gifts,"[2] is its sarcastic comment on the ordinary motives of mean men. Its picture of the plausible, fickle, lip-praising, and time-serving man, who blesseth his friend with a loud voice, rising early in the morning,[3] is a delicate piece of satire. The fragile connections among men, as easily broken as mended pottery, get illustration in the mischief-maker who loves to divide men. "A whisperer separateth chief friends."[4] There is keen irony here over the quality of ordinary friendship, as well as condemnation of the tale-bearer and his sordid soul.

This cynical attitude is so common that we hardly expect such a shrewd book to speak heartily of the possibilities of human friendship. Its object rather is to put youth on its guard against the dangers and pitfalls of social life. It gives sound commercial advice about avoiding becoming surety for a friend. It warns against the tricks, and cheats, and bad faith, which swarmed in the streets of a city then, as they do still. It laughs, a little bitterly, at the thought that friendship can be as common as the eager, generous heart of youth imagines. It almost sneers at the gullibility of men in this whole matter. "He that maketh many friends doeth it to his own destruction."[5]

And yet there is no book, even in classical literature, which so exalts the idea of friendship, and is so anxious to have it truly valued, and carefully kept. The worldly-wise warnings are after all in the interests of true friendship. To condemn hypocrisy is not, as is so often imagined, to condemn religion. To spurn the spurious is not to reject the true. A sneer at folly may be only a covert argument for wisdom. Satire is a negative truth. The unfortunate thing is that most men, who begin with the prudential worldly-wise philosophy, end there. They never

---

1 Proverbs 14:20
2 Proverbs 19:6
3 Proverbs 27:14
4 Proverbs 16:28
5 Proverbs 18:24

get past the sneer. Not so this wise book. In spite of its insight into the weakness of man, in spite of its frank denunciation of the common masquerade of friendship, it speaks of the true kind in words of beauty that have never been surpassed in all the many appraisements of this subject. "A friend loveth at all times, and a brother is born for adversity....Faithful are the wounds of a friend....Ointment and perfume rejoice the heart, so doth the sweetness of a man's friend by hearty counsel. Thine own friend and thy father's friend forsake not."[6] These are not the words of a cynic, who has lost faith in man.

True, this golden friendship is not a common thing to be picked up in the street. It would not be worth much if it were. Like wisdom it must be sought for as for hid treasures, and to keep it demands care and thought. To think that every goose is a swan, that every new comrade is the man of your own heart, is to have a very shallow heart. Every casual acquaintance is not a hero. There are pearls of the heart, which cannot be thrown to swine. Till we learn what a sacred thing a true friendship is, it is futile to speak of the culture of friendship. The man who wears his heart on his sleeve cannot wonder if daws peck at it. There ought to be a sanctuary, to which few receive admittance. It is great innocence, or great folly, and in this connection the terms are almost synonymous, to open our arms to everybody to whom we are introduced. The Book of Proverbs, as a manual on friendship, gives as shrewd and caustic warnings as are needed, but it does not go to the other extreme, and say that all men are liars, that there are no truth and faithfulness to be found. To say so is to speak in haste. "There *is* a friend that sticketh closer than a brother,"[7] says this wisest of books. There is possible such a blessed relationship, a state of love and trust and generous comradehood, where a man feels safe to be himself, because he knows that he will not easily be misunderstood.

The word friendship has been abased by applying it to low and unworthy uses, and so there is plenty of copy still to be got from life

---

6 Proverbs 17:17; 27:6; 27:9-10
7 Proverbs 18:24

by the cynic and the satirist. The sacred name of friend has been bandied about till it runs the risk of losing its true meaning. Rossetti's versicle finds its point in life—

Was it a friend or foe that spread these lies?
'Nay, who but infants question in such wise?
'Twas one of my most intimate enemies.'[8]

It is useless to speak of cultivating the great gift of friendship unless we make clear to ourselves what we mean by a friend. We make connections and acquaintances and call them friends. We have few friendships, because we are not willing to pay the price of friendship.

If we think it is not worth the price, that is another matter, and is quite an intelligible position, but we must not use the word in different senses, and then rail at fate because there is no miracle of beauty and joy about our sort of friendship. Like all other spiritual blessings it comes to all of us at some time or other, and like them is often let slip. We have the opportunities, but we do not make use of them. Most men make friends easily enough: few keep them. They do not give the subject the care, and thought, and trouble, it requires and deserves. We want the pleasure of society, without the duty. We would like to get the good of our friends, without burdening ourselves with any responsibility about keeping them friends. The commonest mistake we make is that we spread our intercourse over a mass, and have no depth of heart left. We lament that we have no staunch and faithful friend, when we have really not expended the love which produces such. We want to reap where we have not sown, the fatuousness of which we should see as soon as it is mentioned. "She that asks her dear five hundred friends" (as Cowper satirically describes a well-known type)[9] cannot expect the exclusive affection, which she has not given.

---

8 Dante Gabriel Rossetti (1828-1882)

9 William Cowper, *The Task*, Book ii (1784)

The secret of friendship is just the secret of all spiritual blessing. The way to get is to give. The selfish in the end can never get anything but selfishness. The hard find hardness everywhere. As you mete, it is meted out to you.

Some men have a genius for friendship. That is because they are open, and responsive, and unselfish. They truly make the most of life; for apart from their special joys, even intellect is sharpened by the development of the affections. No material success in life is comparable to success in friendship. We really do ourselves harm by our selfish standards. There is an old Latin proverb,[10] expressing the worldly view, which says that it is not possible for a man to love and at the same time be wise. This is only true when wisdom is made equal to prudence and selfishness, and when love is made the same. Rather it is never given to a man to be wise in the true and noble sense, until he is carried out of himself in the purifying passion of love, or the generosity of friendship. The self-centred being cannot keep friends, even when he makes them; his selfish sensitiveness is always in the way, like a diseased nerve ready to be irritated.

The culture of friendship is a duty, as every gift represents a responsibility. It is also a necessity; for without watchful care it can no more remain with us than can any other gift. Without culture it is at best only a potentiality. We may let it slip, or we can use it to bless our lives. The miracle of friendship, which came at first with its infinite wonder and beauty, wears off, and the glory fades into the light of common day. The early charm passes, and the soul forgets the first exaltation. We are always in danger of mistaking the common for the commonplace. We must not look upon it merely as the great luxury of life, or it will cease to be even that. It begins with emotion, but if it is to remain it must become a habit. Habit is fixed when an accustomed thing is organized into life; and, whatever be the genesis of friendship, it must become a habit, or it is in danger of passing away as other impressions have done before.

---

10 *Non simul cuiquam conceditur, amare et sapere.*

Friendship needs delicate handling. We can ruin it by stupid blundering at the very birth, and we can kill it by neglect. It is not every flower that has vitality enough to grow in stony ground. Lack of reticence, which is only the outward sign of lack of reverence, is responsible for the death of many a fair friendship. Worse still, it is often blighted at the very beginning by the insatiable desire for piquancy in talk, which can forget the sacredness of confidence. "An acquaintance grilled, scored, devilled, and served with mustard and cayenne pepper, excites the appetite; whereas a slice of cold friend with currant jelly is but a sickly, unrelishing meat."[11] Nothing is given to the man who is not worthy to possess it, and the shallow heart can never know the joy of a friendship, for the keeping of which he is not able to fulfill the essential conditions. Here also it is true that from the man that hath not, is taken away even that which he hath.

The method for the culture of friendship finds its best and briefest summary in the Golden Rule. To do to, and for, your friend what you would have him do to, and for, you, is a simple compendium of the whole duty of friendship. The very first principle of friendship is that it is a mutual thing, as among spiritual equals, and therefore it claims reciprocity, mutual confidence and faithfulness. There must be sympathy to keep in touch with each other, but sympathy needs to be constantly exercised. It is a channel of communication, which has to be kept open, or it will soon be clogged and closed.

The practice of sympathy may mean the cultivation of similar tastes, though that will almost naturally follow from the fellowship. But to cultivate similar tastes does not imply either absorption of one of the partners, or the identity of both. Rather, part of the charm of the intercourse lies in the difference, which exists in the midst of agreement. What is essential is that there should be a real desire and a genuine effort to understand each other. It is well worth while taking pains to preserve a relationship so full of blessing to both.

---

11 William Makepeace Thackeray, *Roundabout Papers* (1860-1863)

Here, as in all connections among men, there is also ample scope for patience. When we think of our own need for constant exercise of this virtue, we will admit its necessity for others. After the first flush of communion has passed, we must see in a friend things which detract from his worth, and perhaps things which irritate us. This is only to say that no man is perfect. With tact, and tenderness, and patience, it may be given us to help to remove what may be flaws in a fine character, and in any case it is foolishness to forget the great virtues of our friend in fretful irritation at a few blemishes. We can keep the first ideal in our memory, even if we know that it is not yet an actual fact. We must not let our intercourse be coarsened, but must keep it sweet and delicate, that it may remain a refuge from the coarse world, a sanctuary where we leave criticism outside, and can breathe freely.

Trust is the first requisite for making a friend. How can we be anything but alone, if our attitude to men is one of armed neutrality, if we are suspicious, and assertive, and querulous, and over-cautious in our advances? Suspicion kills friendship. There must be some magnanimity and openness of mind, before a friendship can be formed. We must be willing to give ourselves freely and unreservedly.

Some find it easier than others to make advances, because they are naturally more trustful. A beginning has to be made somehow, and if we are moved to enter into personal association with another, we must not be too cautious in displaying our feeling. If we stand off in cold reserve, the ice, which trembled to thawing, is gripped again by the black hand of frost. There may be a golden moment which has been lost through foolish reserve. We are so afraid of giving ourselves away cheaply—and it is a proper enough feeling, the value of which we learn through sad experience—but on the whole perhaps the warm nature, which acts on impulse, is of a higher type, than the over-cautious nature, ever on the watch lest it commit itself. We can do nothing with each other, we cannot even do business with each other, without a certain amount of trust. Much more necessary is it in the beginning of a deeper intercourse.

And if trust is the first requisite for making a friend, *faithfulness* is the first requisite for keeping him. The way to have a friend is to be a friend. Faithfulness is the fruit of trust. We must be ready to lay hold of every opportunity which occurs of serving our friend. Life is made up to most of us of little things, and many a friendship withers through sheer neglect. Hearts are alienated, because each is waiting for some great occasion for displaying affection. The great spiritual value of friendship is the opportunity it affords for service, and if these are neglected it is only to be expected that the gift should be taken from us. Friendship, which begins with sentiment, will not live and thrive on sentiment. There must be loyalty, which finds expression in service. It is not the greatness of the help, or the intrinsic value of the gift, which gives it its worth, but the evidence it is of love and thoughtfulness.

Attention to detail is the secret of success in every sphere of life, and little kindnesses, little acts of considerateness, little appreciations, little confidences, are all that most of us are called on to perform, but they are all that are needed to keep a friendship sweet. Such thoughtfulness keeps our sentiment in evidence to both parties. If we never show our kind feeling, what guarantee has our friend, or even ourself, that it exists? Faithfulness in deed is the outward result of constancy of soul, which is the rarest, and the greatness, of virtues. If there has come to us the miracle of friendship, if there is a soul to which our soul has been drawn, it is surely worth while being loyal and true. Through the little occasions for helpfulness, we are training for the great trial, if it should ever come, when the fabric of friendship will be tested to the very foundation. The culture of friendship, and its abiding worth, never found nobler expression than in the beautiful proverb, "A friend loveth at all times, and is a brother born for adversity."[12]

Most men do not deserve such a gift from heaven. They look upon it as a convenience, and accept the privilege of love, without the

---

12 Proverbs 17:17

responsibility of it. They even use their friends for their own selfish purposes, and so never have true friends. Some men shed friends at every step they rise in the social scale. It is mean and contemptible to merely use men, so long as they further one's personal interests. But there is a nemesis on such heartlessness. To such can never come the ecstasy and comfort of mutual trust. This worldly policy can never truly succeed. It stands to reason that they cannot have brothers born for adversity, and cannot count on the joy of the love that loveth at all times; for they do not possess the quality which secures it. To act on the worldly policy, to treat a friend as if he might become an enemy, is of course to be friendless. To sacrifice a tried and trusted friend for any personal advantage of gain or position, is to deprive our own heart of the capacity for friendship.

The passion for novelty will sometimes lead a man to act like this. Some shallow minds are ever afflicted by a craving for new experiences. They sit very loosely to the past. They are the easy victims of the untried, and yearn perpetually for novel sensations. In this matter of friendship they are ready to forsake the old for the new. They are always finding a swan in every goose they meet. They have their reward in a widowed heart. Says Shakespeare in his great manner:

> *Thy friends thou hast and their adoption tried*
> *Grapple them to thy soul with hoops of steel,*
> *But do not dull thy palm with entertainment*
> *Of each new-hatched, unfledged comrade.*[13]

The culture of friendship must pass into the consecration of friendship, if it is to reach its goal. It is a natural evolution. Friendship cannot be permanent unless it becomes spiritual. There must be fellowship in the deepest things of the soul, community in the highest thoughts, sympathy with the best endeavours. We are bartering with priceless boon, if we are looking on friendship merely as a

---

13 Polonius to Laertes in William Shakespeare, *Hamlet*, Act I, Scene ii.

luxury, and not as a spiritual opportunity. It is, or can be, an occasion for growing in grace, for learning love, for training the heart to patience and faith, for knowing the joy of humble service. We are throwing away our chance, if we are not striving to be an inspiring and healthful environment to our friend. We are called to be our best to our friend, that he may be his best to us, bringing out what is highest and deepest in the nature of both.

The culture of friendship is one of the approved instruments of culture of the heart, without which a man has not truly come into his kingdom. It is often only the beginning, but through tender and careful culture it may be an education for the larger life of love. It broadens out in ever-widening circles, from the particular to the general, and from the general to the universal—from the individual to the social, and from the social to God. The test of religion is ultimately a very simple one: If we do not love those whom we have seen, we cannot love those whom we have not seen. All our sentiment about people at a distance, and our heart-stirrings for the distressed and oppressed, and our prayers for the heathen, are point-less and fraudulent, if we are neglecting the occasions for service lying to our hand. If we do not love our brethren here, how can we love our brethren elsewhere, except as a pious sentimentality? And if we do not love those we have seen, how can we love God whom we have not seen?[14]

This is the highest function of friendship, and is the reason why it needs thoughtful culture. We should be led to God by the joy of our lives as well as by the sorrow, by the light as well as by the dark-ness, by human intercourse as well as by human loneliness. He is the Giver of every good gift. We wound his heart of love, when we sin against love. The more we know of Christ's spirit, and the more we think of the meaning of God's fathomless grace, the more will we be convinced that the way to please the Father and to follow the Son is to cultivate the graces of kindliness and gentleness and tenderness,

---

14 1 John 4:20

to give ourselves to the culture of the heart. Not in the ecclesiastical arena, not in polemic for a creed, not in self-assertion and disputings, do we please our Master best, but in the simple service of love. To seek the good of men is to seek the glory of God. They are not two things, but one and the same. To be a strong hand in the dark to another in the time of need, to be a cup of strength to a human soul in a crisis of weakness, is to know the glory of life. To be a true friend, saving his faith in man, and making him believe in the existence of love, is to save his faith in God. And such service is possible for all. We need not wait for the great occasion and for the exceptional opportunity. We can never be without our chance, if we are ready to keep the miracle of love green in our hearts by humble service.

The primal duties shine aloft like stars.
The charities that soothe, and heal, and bless,
Are scattered at the feet of man, like flowers. [15]

---

15 William Wordsworth, *The Excursion*, Book IX (1814)

Two are better than one; because they have a good reward for their labour. For if they fall, the one will lift up his fellow: but woe to him that is alone when he falleth; for he hath not another to help him up....And if one prevail against him, two shall withstand him; and a threefold cord is not quickly broken.

~ ECCLESIASTES 4:9–10,12

O friend, my bosom said,
Through thee alone the sky is arched,
Through thee the rose is red,
All things through thee take nobler form
And look beyond the earth,
And is the mill-round of our fate,
A sun-path in thy worth.
Me too thy nobleness has taught
To master my despair;
The fountains of my hidden life
Are through thy friendship fair.

~ RALPH WALDO EMERSON

Chapter 3

The Fruits of Friendship

I n our utilitarian age things are judged by their practical value. Men ask of everything, What is its use? Nothing is held to be outside criticism, neither the law because of its authority, nor religion because of its sacredness. Every relationship in life also has been questioned, and is asked to show the reason of its existence. Even some relationships like marriage, for long held to be above question, are put into the crucible.

On the whole it is a good spirit, though it can be abused and carried to an absurd extreme. Criticism is inevitable, and ought to be welcomed, provided we are careful about the true standard to apply. When we judge a thing by its use, we must not have a narrow view of what utility is. Usefulness to man is not confined to mere material values. The common standards of the marketplace cannot be applied to the whole of life. The things which cannot be bought cannot be sold, and the keenest valuator would be puzzled to put a price on some of these unmarketable wares.

When we seek to show what are the fruits of friendship, we may be said to put ourselves in line with the critical spirit of our age. But even if it were proven that a man could make more of his life materially by himself, if he gave no hostages to fortune, it would not follow that it is well to disentangle oneself from the common bonds; for our *caveat* would here apply, that utility is larger than mere material gain.

But even from this point of view friendship justifies itself. Two are better than one; for they have a good reward for their labour. The principle of association in business is now accepted universally. It is found even to pay, to share work and profit. Most of the world's business is done by companies, or partnerships, or associated endeavour of some kind. And the closer the intimacy between the men so engaged, the intimacy of common desires and common purposes, and, if possible, friendship, the better the chance there is for success. Two are better than one from the point of view even of the reward of each, and a threefold cord is not quickly broken, when a single strand would snap.

When men first learned, even in its most rudimentary sense, that union is strength, the dawn of civilization began. For offence and for defence, the principle of association early proved itself the fittest for survival. The future is always with Isaac, not with Ishmael—with Jacob, not with Esau. In everything this is seen, in the struggle of the races, or trade, or ideas. Even as a religious method to make an impact on the world, it is true. John of the Desert touched here a life, and there a life; Jesus of Nazareth, seeking disciples, founding a society, moved the world to its heart.

It is not necessary to labour this point, that two are better than one, to a commercial age like ours, which, whatever it does not know, at least knows its arithmetic. We would say that it is self-evident that by the law of addition it is double, and by the law of multiplication twice the number. But it is not so exact as that, nor so self-evident. When we are dealing with men, our ready-reckoner rules do not work out correctly. In this region one and one are not always two. They are sometimes more than two, and sometimes less than two. Union of all kinds, which may be strength, may be weakness. It was not till Gideon weeded out his army, once and twice, that he was promised victory. The fruits of friendship may be corrupting, and unspeakably evil to the life. The reward of the labour of two may be less than that of one. The boy pulling a barrow is lucky if he get another boy to shove behind, but if the boy behind not only ceases to shove, but sits on the barrow, the last end is worse than the first. A threefold cord with two of the strands rotten is worse than a single sound strand, for it deceives into putting too much weight on it.

In social economics it is evident that society is not merely the sum of the units that compose it. Two are better than one, not merely because the force is doubled. It may even be said that two are better than two. Two together mean more than two added singly; for a new element is introduced which increases the power of each individually. When the man Friday came into the life of Robinson Crusoe, he brought with him a great deal more than his own individual value, which with his lower civilization would not be very much. But to Robinson Crusoe he represented society, and all the possibilities of social polity. It meant also the satisfaction of the social instincts, the play of the affections, and made Crusoe a different man. The two living together were more than the two living on different desert islands.

The truth of this strange contradiction of the multiplication table is seen in the relationship of friends. Each gives to the other, and each receives, and the fruit of the intercourse is more than either in himself possesses. Every individual relationship has contact with a universal. To reach out to the fuller life of love is a divine enchantment, because it leads to more than itself, and is the open door into the mystery of life. We feel ourselves united to the race and no longer isolated units, but in the sweep of the great social forces which mould mankind. Every bond which binds man to man is a new argument for the permanence of life itself, and gives a new insight into its meaning. Love is the pledge and the promise of the future.

Besides this cosmic and perhaps somewhat shadowy benefit, there are many practical fruits of friendship to the individual. These may be classified and sub-divided almost endlessly, and indeed in every special friendship the fruits of it will differ according to the character and closeness of the tie, and according to the particular gifts of each of the partners. One man can give to his friend some quality of sympathy, or some kind of help, or can supply some social need which is lacking in his character or circumstances. Perhaps it is not possible to get a better division of the subject than the three noble fruits of friendship which Bacon enumerates—peace in the affections, support of the judgment and aid in all actions and occasions.[1]

First of all there is the *satisfaction of the heart*. We cannot live a self-centred life, without feeling that we are missing the true glory of life. We were made for social intercourse, if only that the highest qualities of our nature might have an opportunity for development. The joy, which a true friendship gives, reveals the existence of the want of it, perhaps previously unfelt. It is a sin against ourselves to let our affections wither. This sense of incompleteness is an argument in favour of its possible satisfaction; our need is an argument for its fulfillment. Our hearts demand love, as truly as our bodies demand food. We cannot live among men, suspicious, and careful of our own interests, and fighting for our own hand, without doing dishonour and hurt to our own nature. To be for ourselves

---

1 Sir Francis Bacon, *Of Friendship* (1625)

puts the whole world against us. To harden our heart hardens the heart of the universe.

We need sympathy, and therefore we crave for friendship. Even the most perfect of the sons of men felt this need of intercourse of heart. Christ, in one aspect the most self-contained of men, showed this human longing all through his life. He ever desired opportunities for enlargement of heart—in his disciples, in an inner circle within the circle, in the household of Bethany. "Will ye also go away?"[2] he asked in the crisis of his career. "Could ye not watch with me one hour?"[3] he sighed in his great agony. He was perfectly human, and therefore felt the lack of friendship. The higher our relationships with each other are, the closer is the intercourse demanded. Highest of all in the things of the soul, we feel that the true Christian life cannot be lived in the desert, but must be a life among men, and this because it is a life of joy as well as of service. We feel that, for the rounding of our life and the completion of our powers, we need intercourse with our kind. Stunted affections dwarf the whole man. We live by admiration, hope, and love, and these can be developed only in the social life.

The sweetest and most stable pleasures also are never selfish. They are derived from fellowship, from common tastes, and mutual sympathy. Sympathy is not a quality merely needed in adversity. It is needed as much when the sun shines. Indeed, it is more easily obtained in adversity than in prosperity. It is comparatively easy to sympathize with a friend's *failure*, when we are not so true-hearted about his success. When a man is down in his luck, he can be sure of at least a certain amount of good-fellowship to which he can appeal. It is difficult to keep a little touch of malice, or envy, out of congratulations. It is sometimes easier to weep with those who weep, than to rejoice with those who rejoice.[4] This difficulty is felt not

---

2 John 6:67
3 Matthew 26:40
4 Romans 12:15

with people above us, or with little connection with us, but with our equals. When a friend succeeds, there may be a certain regret which has not always an evil root, but is due to a fear that he is getting beyond our reach, passing out of our sphere, and perhaps will not need or desire our friendship so much as before. It is a dangerous feeling to give way to, but up to a certain point it is natural and legitimate. A perfect friendship would not have room for such grudging sympathy, but would rejoice more for the other's success than for his own. The envious, jealous man never can be a friend. His mean spirit of detraction and insinuating ill-will kills friendship at its birth. Plutarch records a witty remark about Plistarchus, who was told that a notorious railer has spoken well of him. "I'll lay my life," said he, "somebody has told him I am dead, for he can speak well of no man living."[5]

For true satisfaction of the heart, there must be a fount of sympathy from which to draw in all the vicissitudes of life. Sorrow asks for sympathy, aches to let its griefs be known and shared by a kindred spirit. To find such, is to dispel the loneliness from life. To have a heart which we can trust, and into which we can pour our griefs and our doubts and our fears, is already to take the edge from grief, and the sting from doubt, and the shade from fear.

Joy also demands that its joy should be shared. The man who has found his sheep that was lost calls together his neighbours, and bids them rejoice with him because he has found the sheep that was lost.[6] Joy is more social than grief. Some forms of grief desire only to creep away into solitude like a wounded beast to its lair, to suffer alone and to die alone. But joy finds its counterpart in the sunshine and the flowers and the birds and the little children, and enters easily into all the movements of life. Sympathy will respond to a friend's gladness, as well as vibrate to his grief. A simple generous friendship will thus add to the joy, and will divide the sorrow.

---

5 Plutarch, *Laconic Apophthegms*
6 Luke 15:5-6

The religious life, in spite of all the unnatural experiments of monasticism and all its kindred ascetic forms, is pre-eminently a life of friendship. It is individual in its root, and social in its fruits. It is when two or three are gathered together that religion becomes a fact for the world. The joy of religion will not be hid and buried in a man's own heart. "Come, see a man that told me all that ever I did,"[7] is the natural outcome of the first wonder and the first faith. It spreads from soul to soul by the impact of soul on soul, from the original impact of the great soul of God.

Christ's ideal is the ideal of a Kingdom, men banded together in a common cause, under common laws, serving the same purpose of love. It is meant to take effect upon man in all his social relationships, in the home, in the city, in the state. Its greatest triumphs have been made through friendship, and it in turn has ennobled and sanctified the bond. The growth of the Kingdom depends on the sanctified working of the natural ties among men. It was so at the very start; John the Baptist pointed out the Christ to John the future Apostle and to Andrew; Andrew findeth his own brother Simon Peter; Philip findeth Nathanael;[8] and so society through its network of relations took into its heart the new message. The man who has been healed must go and tell those who are at home, must declare it to his friends, and seek that they also should share in his great discovery.

The very existence of the church as a body of believers is due to this necessity of our nature, which demands opportunity for the interchange of Christian sentiment. The deeper the feeling, the greater is the joy of sharing it with another. There is a strange felicity, a wondrous enchantment, which comes from true intimacy of heart, and close communion of soul, and the result is more than mere fleeting joy. When it is shared in the deepest thoughts and highest aspirations, when it is built on a common faith, and lives by a common hope, it brings perfect peace. No friendship has done its work until

---

7 John 4:29
8 John 1:40-45

it reaches the supremest satistfaction of spiritual communion.

Besides the satisfaction of the heart, friendship also gives *satisfaction of the mind*. Most men have a certain natural diffidence in coming to conclusions and forming opinions for themselves. We rarely feel confident, until we have secured the agreement of others in whom we trust. There is always a personal equation in all our judgments, so that we feel that they require to be amended by comparison with those of others. Doctors ask for a consultation, when a case becomes critical. We all realize the advantage of taking counsel. To ask for advice is a benefit, whether we follow the advice or no. Indeed, the best benefit often comes from the opportunity of testing our own opinion and finding it valid. Sometimes the very statement of the case is enough to prove it one thing or the other. An advantage is reaped from a sympathetic listener, apart altogether whether our friend is able to elucidate the matter by his special sagacity or experience. Friends in counsel gain much intellectually. They acquire something approaching to a standard of judgment, and are enabled to classify opinions, and to make up the mind more accurately and securely. Through talking a subject over with another, one gets fresh side-lights into it, new avenues open up, and the whole question becomes larger and richer. Bacon says,

> *Friendship maketh daylight in the understanding, out of darkness and confusion of thoughts: neither is this to be understood only of faithful counsel, which a man receiveth from his friend; but before you come to that, certain it is, that whosoever hath his mind fraught with many thoughts, his wits and understanding do clarify and break up in the communicating and discoursing with another; he tosseth his thoughts more easily; he marshalleth them more orderly; he seeth how they look when they are turned into words; finally he waxeth wiser than himself; and that more by an hour's discourse than by a day's meditation.[9]*

---

9 Sir Francis Bacon, *Of Friendship* (1625)

We must have been struck with the brilliancy of our own conversation and the profundity of our own thoughts, when we shared them with one, with whom we were in sympathy at the time. The brilliancy was not ours; it was the reflex action which was the result of the communion. That is why the effect of different people upon us is different, one making us creep into our shell and making us unable almost to utter a word; another through some strange magnetism enlarging the bounds of our whole being and drawing the best out of us. The true insight after all is love. It clarifies the intellect, and opens the eyes to much that was obscure.

Besides the subjective influence, there may be the great gain of honest counsel. A faithful friend can be trusted not to speak merely soft words of flattery. It is often the spectator who sees most of the game, and, if the spectator is at the same time keenly interested in us, he can have a more unbiased opinion than we can possibly have. He may have to say that which may wound our self-esteem; he may have to speak for correction rather than for commendation; but "Faithful are the wounds of a friend."[10] The flatterer will take good care not to offend our susceptibilities by too many shocks of wholesome truth-telling; but a friend will seek our good, even if he must say a thing we hate to hear at the time.

This does not mean that a friend should always be what is called plain-spoken. Many take advantage of what they call a true interest in our welfare, in order to rub gall into our wounds. The man who boasts of his frankness and of his hatred of flattery, is usually not frank—but only brutal. A true friend will never needlessly hurt, but also will never let slip occasions through cowardice. To speak the truth in love takes off the edge of unpleasantness,[11] which so often is found in truth-speaking. And however the wound may smart, in the end we are thankful for the faithfulness which directed it. "Let the righteous smite me; it shall be a kindness: and let him reprove me;

---

10 Proverbs 27:6
11 Ephesians 4:15

39

it shall be an excellent oil, which shall not break my head."[12]

In our relations with each other, there is usually more advantage to be reaped from friendly encouragement, than from friendly correction. True criticism does not consist, as so many critics seem to think, in depreciation, but in appreciation; in putting oneself sympathetically in another's position, and seeking to value the real worth of his work. There are more lives spoiled by undue harshness, than by undue gentleness. More good work is lost from want of appreciation than from too much of it; and certainly it is not the function of friendship to do the critic's work. Unless carefully repressed, such a spirit becomes censorious, or, worse still, spiteful, and has often been the means of losing a friend. It is possible to be kind, without giving crooked counsel, or oily flattery; and it is possible to be true, without magnifying faults, and indulging in cruel rebukes.

Besides the joy of friendship, and its aid in matters of cousel, a third of its noble fruits is *the direct help it can give us in the difficulties of life.* It gives strength to the character. It sobers and steadies through the responsibility for each other which it means. When men face the world together, and ready to stand shoulder to shoulder, the sense of comradeship makes each strong. This help may not often be called into play, but just to know that it is there if needed is a great comfort, to know that if one falls the other will lift him up. The very word friendship suggests kindly help and aid in distress. Shakespeare applies the word in *King Lear* to an inanimate thing with this meaning of helpfulness:

> *Gracious my lord, hard by here is a hovel;*
> *Some* friendship *will it lend you 'gainst the tempest.*[13]

Sentiment does not amount to much, if it is not an inspiring force to lead to gentle and generous deeds, when there is need. The fight is not so hard, when we know that we are not alone, but that

---

12 Psalm 141:5

13 William Shakespeare, *King Lear*, Act III, Scene ii

there are some who think of us, and pray for us, and would gladly help us if they got the opportunity.

Comradeship is one of the finest facts, and one of the strongest forces in life. A mere strong man, however capable, and however singly successful, is of little account by himself. There is no glamour of romance in his career. The kingdom of romance belongs to David, not to Samson—to David, with his eager, impetuous, affectionate nature, for whom three men went in the jeopardy of life to bring him a drink of water; and all for love of him. It is not the self-centred, self-contained hero, who lays hold of us; it is ever the comradeship of heroes. Dumas' three Musketeers (and the Gascon who made a greater fourth), with their oath, "Each for all, and all for each," inherit that kingdom of romance, with all that ever have been tied in bands of love.[14]

Robertson of Brighton in one of his letters tells how a friend of his had, through cowardice or carelessness, missed an opportunity of putting him right on a point with which he was charged, and so left him defenceless against a slander. With his native sweetness of soul, he contents himself with the exclamation, "How rare it is to have a friend who will defend you thoroughly and boldly!" Yet that is just one of the loyal things a friend can do, sometimes when it would be impossible for a man himself to do himself justice with others. Some things, needful to be said or done under certain circumstances, cannot be undertaken without indelicacy by the person concerned, and the keen instinct of a friend should tell him that he is needed. A little thoughtfulness would often suggest things that could be done for our friends, that would make them feel that the tie which binds us to them is a real one. That man is rich indeed, who possesses thoughtful, tactful friends, with whom he feels safe when present, and in whose hands his honour is secure when absent. If there be no loyalty, there can be no great friendship. Most of our friendships lack the distinction of greatness, because we are not ready for little acts of service. Without these our love dwindles down to a mere

---

14 Alexandre Dumas, *The Three Musketeers* (1844)

sentiment, and ceases to be the inspiring force for good to both lives, which it was at the beginning.

The aid we may receive from friendship may be of an even more powerful, because of a more subtle, nature than material help. It may be a safeguard against temptation. The recollection of a friend whom we admire is a great force to save us from evil, and to prompt us to good. The thought of his sorrow in any moral breakdown of ours will often nerve us to stand firm. What would my friend think of me, if I did this, or consented to this meanness? Could I look him in the face again, and meet the calm pure gaze of his eye? Would it not be a blot on our friendship, and draw a veil over our intercourse? No friendship is worth the name which does not elevate, and does not help to nobility of conduct and to strength of character. It should give a new zest to duty, and a new inspiration to all that is good.

Influence is the greatest of all human gifts, and we all have it in some measure. There are some to whom we are something, if not everything. There are some, who are grappled to us with hoops of steel. There are some, over whom we have ascendency, or at least to whom we have access, who have opened the gates of the City of Mansoul to us,[15] some we can sway with a word, a touch, a look. It must always be a solemn thing for a man to ask what he has done with this dread power of influence. For what has our friend been indebted to us—for good or evil? Have we put on his armour, and sent him out with courage and strength to the battle? Or have we dragged him down from the heights to which he once aspired? We are face to face here with the tragic possibilities of human intercourse. In all friendship we open the gates of the city, and those who have entered must be either allies in the fight, or treacherous foes.

All the fruits of friendship, be they blessed or baneful, spring from this root of influence, and influence in the long run is the impress of our real character on other lives. Influence cannot rise

---

15 Reference from John Bunyan's *The Holy War* (1682)

above the level of our lives. The result of our friendship on others will ultimately be conditioned by the sort of persons we are. It adds a very sacred responsibility to life. Here, as in other regions, a good tree bringeth forth good fruit, but a corrupt tree bringeth forth evil fruit.[16]

---

16 Matthew 7:17

*If thou findest a good man, rise up early in the morning to
go to him, and let thy feet wear the steps of his door.*
~ ECCLESIASTICUS 6:36

Whereof the man, that with me trod
 This planet, was a noble type,
Appearing ere the times were ripe,
 That friend of mine who lives with God.
~ ALFRED, LORD TENNYSON

Chapter 4

The Choice of Friendship

Our responsibility for our friendships is not confined to making sure that our influence over others is for good. We have also a duty to ourselves. As we possess the gift of influence over others, so we in turn are affected by every life which touches ours. Influence is like an atmosphere exhaled by each separate personality. Some men seem neutral and colourless, with no atmosphere to speak of. Some have a bad atmosphere, like the rank poisonous odour of noxious weeds, breeding malaria. If our moral sense were only keen and true, we would instinctively know them, as some children do, and dread their company. Others have a good atmosphere; we can breathe there in safety, and have a joyful sense of security. With some of these it is a local delicate environment, sweet, suggestive, like the aroma of wild violets: we have to look, and sometimes to stoop, to get into its range. With some it is like a Scotch pine forest, or a eucalyptus grove of warmer climes, which perfumes a whole countryside. It is well to know such, Christ's little ones and Christ's great ones. They put oxygen into the moral atmosphere and we breathe more freely for it. They give us new insight, and fresh courage, and purer faith, and by the impulse of their example inspire us to nobler life.

There is nothing so important as the choice of friendship; for it both reflects character and affects it. A man is known by the company he keeps.[1] This is an infallible test; for his thoughts, and desires, and ambitions, and loves are revealed here. He gravitates naturally to his congenial sphere. And it affects character; for it is the atmosphere he breathes. It enters his blood and makes the circuit of his veins. "All love assimilates to what it loves."[2] A man is moulded into likeness of the lives that come nearest him. It is at the point of the emotions that he is most impressionable. The material surroundings, the outside lot of a man, affects him, but after all that is mostly on the outside; for the higher functions of life may be served in almost any external circumstances. But the environment of other lives, the communion of other souls, are far more potent facts. The nearer people are to each other, and the less disguise there is in their relationship the more invariably will the law of spiritual environment act.

It seems a tragedy that people, who see each other as they are, become like each other; and often it is a tragedy. But the law carries as much hope in it as despair. If through it evil works havoc,

---

1 Henry Smith, *A Preparative to Marriage* (1591)
2 St. John of the Cross, *The Dark Night of the Soul*, Book II, Ch. xx (*circa* 1580)

through it also good persists. If we are hindered by the weakness of our associates, we are often helped by their goodness and sweetness. Contact with a strong nature inspires us with strength. Someone once asked Kingsley what was the secret of his strong joyous life, and he answered, "I had a friend."[3] If every evil man is a centre of contagion, every good man is a centre of healing. He provides an environment in which others can see God. Goodness creates an atmosphere for other souls to be good. It is a priestly garment that has virtue even for the finger that touches it. The earth has its salt, and the world has its light, in the sweet souls, and winsome lives, and Christ-like characters to be found in it. The choice of friends is therefore one of the most serious affairs in life, just because a man becomes moulded into the likeness of what he loves in his friend.

From the purely selfish standard, every fresh tie we form means giving a new hostage to fortune, and adding a new risk to our happiness. Apart from any moral evil, every intimacy is a danger of another blow to the heart. But if we desire fulness of life, we cannot help ourselves. A man may make many a friendship to his own hurt, but the isolated life is a greater danger still. *Societas est mater discordiarum*, which Scott in his humorous pathetic account of the lawsuits of Peter Peebles versus Plainstanes in *Redgauntlet*,[4] translates, "Partnership oft makes pleaship." Every relationship means risk, but we must take the risk; for while nearly all our sorrows come from our connection with others, nearly all our joys have the same source. We cannot help ourselves; for it is part of the great discipline of life. Rather, we need knowledge, and care, and forethought to enable us to make the best use of the necessities of our nature. And foremost of these for importance is our choice of friends.

We may err on the one side by being too cautious, and too exclusive in our attachments. We may be supercilious, and disdainful in our estimate of men. Contempt always blinds the eyes. Every man

---

3 Elizabeth Barrett Browning to novelist Charles Kingsley
4 Sir Walter Scott, *Redgauntlet* (1824)

is vulnerable somewhere, if only like Achilles in the heel. The true secret of insight is not contempt, but sympathy. Such disdain usually means putting all the eggs into one basket, when a smash spells ruin.

The other extreme is the attitude, which easily makes many friends, without much consideration of quality. We know the type of man, who is friendly with everybody, and a friend of none. He is "Hail fellow well met!" with every passing stranger, a boon companion of every wayfarer. He takes up with every sort of casual comrade, and seeks to be on good terms with everybody. He makes what is called, with a little contempt, good company, and is a favourite on all light occasions. His affections spread themselves out over a large expanse. He is easily consoled for a loss, and easily attracted by a new attachment. And as he deals, so is he dealt with. Many like him; few quite trust him. He makes many friends, and is not particular about their quality. The law of spiritual environment plays upon him with its relentless force. He gives himself away too cheaply, and opens himself to all sorts of influence. He is constantly laying himself in the way of temptation. His mind takes on the opinions of his set: his character assimilates itself to the forces that act on it. The evil example of some of his intimates gradually breaks down the barriers of past training and teaching. The desire to please a crowd means that principle is let slip, and conscience ceases to be the standard of action. His very friends are not true friends, being mostly of the fair-weather quality.

Though it may seem difficult to avoid either of these two extremes, it will not do to refuse to choose at all, and leave things to chance. We drift into many of our connections with men, but the art of seamanship is tested by sailing not by drifting. The subject of the choice of friendship is not advanced much by just letting them choose us. That is to become the victim, not the master of our circumstances. And while it is true that we are acted on as much as we act, and are chosen as much as we choose, it is not permitted to any one merely to be passive, except at great cost.

At the same time in the mystery of friendship we cannot say that we went about with a touchstone testing all we met, till we found the ore that would respond to our particular magnet. It is not that we said to ourselves, "Go to, we will choose a friend," and straightway made a distinct election to the vacant throne of our heart. From one point of view we were absolutely passive. Things arranged themselves without effort, and by some subtle affinity we learned that we had gained a friend. The history of every true friendship is the brief description of Emerson, "My friends have come to me unsought; the great God gave them to me."[5] There was an element of necessity in this, as in all crises of life.

Does it therefore seem absurd and useless to speak about the choice of friendship at all? By no means, because the principles we set before ourselves will determine the kind of friends we have, as truly as if the whole initiative lay with us. We are chosen for the same reason for which we would choose. To try to separate the two processes is to make the same futile distinction, on a lower scale, so often made between choosing God and being chosen by him. It is futile, because the distinction cannot be maintained.

Besides, the value of having some definite principle by which to test friendship is not confined to the positive attachments made. The necessity for a system of selection is largely due to the necessity for rejection. The good and great intimacies of our life will perhaps come to us, as the wind bloweth, we cannot tell how. But by regulating our course wisely, we will escape from hampering our life by mistakes, and weakening it with false connections. We ought to be courteous, and kind, and gentle with all, but not to all can we open the sanctuary of our heart.

We have a graduated scale of intimacy, from introduction, and nodding acquaintance, and speaking acquaintance, through an endless series of kinds of intercourse to the perfect friendship. In counting up our gains and our resources, we cannot give them all the same value, without deceiving ourselves. To expect loyalty and devotion from all alike is to court disappointment. Most misanthropical and

---

5 Ralph Waldo Emerson, *Friendship* (1841)

cynical estimates of man are due to this mingled ignorance and conceit. We cannot look for undying affection from the crowd we may happen to have entertained to dinner, or have rubbed shoulders with at business resorts or at social gatherings. Many men in life, as many are depicted in literature, have played the misanthrope,[6] because they have discovered through adversity how many of their associates were fair-weather friends. In their prosperity they encouraged toadying and sycophancy.[7] They liked to have hangers-on, who would flatter, and when the east wind blows they are indignant that their circle should prefer to avoid it.

Shakespeare's Timon of Athens is a typical misanthrope in his virtuous indignation at the cat-like love of men for comfort.[8] In his prosperity crowds of glass-faced flatterers bent before him, and were made rich in Timon's nod. He wasted his substance in presents and hospitality, and bred a fine race of parasites and trencher-friends. When he spent all and began to be in want, no man gave unto him. The winter shower drove away the summer flies. He had loved the reputation for splendid liberality, and lavish generosity, and had sought to be a little god among men, bestowing favours and receiving homage, all of which was only a more subtle form of selfishness. When the brief day of prosperity passed, men shut their doors against the setting sun. The smooth and smiling crowd dropped off with a shrug, and Timon went to the other extreme of misanthropy, declaimed against friendship, and cursed men for their ingratitude. But after all he got what he had paid for. He thought he had been buying the hearts of men, and found that he had only bought their mouths, and tongues, and eyes.

"He that loves to be flattered is worthy of the flatterer."[9] For moral value there is not much to choose between them. Rats are said to

---

6 Or avoided human company.

7 Or self-seeking flattery.

8 William Shakespeare, *Timon of Athens* (1623)

9 Shakespeare, *Timon of Athens*, Act I, Scene i

desert the sinking ship, which is not to be wondered at in rats. The choice of friendship does not mean the indiscriminate acceptance of all who are willing to assume the name of friend. A touch of east wind is good, not only to weed out the false and test the true, but also to brace a man to the stern realities of life. When we find that some of our intimates are dispersed by adversity, instead of raving against the world's ingratitude like Timon, we should be glad that now we know whom exactly we can trust.

Another common way of choosing friends, and one which also meets with its own fitting reward, is the selfish method of valuing men according to their usefulness to us. To add to their credit, or reputation, some are willing to include anybody in their list of intimates. For business purposes even, men will sometimes run risks, by endangering the peace of their home and the highest interests of those they love; they are ready to introduce into their family circle men whom they distrust morally, because they think they can make some gain out of the connection.

All the stupid snobbishness, and mean tuft-hunting so common, are due to the same desire to make use of people in some way or other. It is an abuse of the word friendship to apply it to such social scrambling. Of course, even tuft-hunting may be only a perverted desire after what we think the best, a longing to get near those we consider of nobler nature and larger mind than common associates. It may be an instinctive agreement with Plato's definition of the wise man, as ever wanting to be with him who is better than himself. But in its usual form it becomes an unspeakable degradation, inducing servility, and lick-spittle humility, and all the vices of the servile mind. There can never be true friendship without self-respect, and unless soul meets soul free from self-seeking. If we had higher standards for ourselves, if we lived to God and not to men, we would also find that in the truest sense we would live with men. We need not go out of our way to ingratiate ourselves with anybody. Nothing can make up for the loss of independence and native dignity of soul. It is not for a man, made in the image of God, to grovel, and demean himself before his fellow-creatures.

After all it defeats itself; for there can only be friendship *between equals*. This does not mean equals in what is called social position, nor even in intellectual attainments, though these naturally have weight, but it means equality which has a spiritual source. "Can two walk together, except they be agreed?"[10] Nor does it mean identity, nor even likeness. Indeed, for the highest unity there must be difference, the difference of free beings, with will, and conscience, and mind unhampered. We often make much of our differences, forgetting that really we differ, and *can* differ, only because we agree. Without many points of contact there could be no divergence from these. Argument and contradiction of opinion are the outcome of difference, and yet for argument there is needed a common basis. We cannot even discuss, unless we meet on some mental ground common to both disputants. So there may be, nay, for the highest union there *must* be, a great general conformity behind the distinctions, a deep underlying common basis beneath the unlikeness. And for true union of hearts, this equality must have a spiritual source. If then there must be some spiritual affinity, agreement in what is best and highest in each, we can see the futility of most of the selfish attempts to make capital out of our intercourse. Our friends will be, because they must be, our equals. We can never have a nobler intimacy, until we are made fit for it.

All connections based on selfishness, either on personal pleasure or on usefulness, are accidental. They are easily dissolved, because, when the pleasure or the utility ceases, the bond ceases. When the motive of the friendship is removed, the friendship itself disappears. The perfect friendship is grounded on what is permanent, on goodness, on character. It is of much slower growth, since it takes some time to really find out the truly lovable things in a life, but it is lasting, since the foundation is stable.

---

10 Amos 3:3

The most important point, then, about the choice of friendship is that we should know what to reject. Countless attractions come to us on the lower plane. A man may be attracted by what his own conscience tells him to be unworthy. He may have slipped gradually into companionship with some, whose influence is even evil. He may have got, almost without his own will, into a set which is deteriorating his life and character. He knows the fruits of his weakness, in the lowering of the moral tone, in the slackening grip of the conscience, in the looser flow of the blood. He has become pliant in will, feeble in purpose, and flaccid in character. Every man has a duty to himself to be his own best self, and he can never be that under the spell of evil companionship.

Some men mix in doubtful company, and say that they have no Pharisaic exclusiveness, and even sometimes defend themselves by Christ's example, who received sinners and ate with them. The comparison borders on blasphemy. It depends on the purpose, for which sinners are received. Christ never joined in their sin, but went to save them from their sin; and wickedness could not lift its head in his presence. Some seek to be initiated into the mysteries of iniquity, in idle or morbid curiosity, perhaps to write a realistic book, or to see life, as it is called. There is often a prurient desire to explore the tracts of sin, as if information on such subjects meant wisdom. If men are honest with themselves, they will admit that they join the company of sinners, for the relish they have for the sin. We must first obey the moral command to come out from among them and be separate, before it is possible for us to meet them like Christ. Separateness of soul is the law of holiness. Of Christ, of whom it was said that "this man receiveth sinners,"[11] it was also said that he was "separate from sinners."[12] The knowledge of wickedness is not wisdom, neither is the counsel of sinners prudence. Most young men know the temptation here referred to,

---

11 Luke 15:2
12 Hebrews 7:26

the curiosity to learn the hidden things, and to have the air of those who know the world.

If we have gone wrong here, and have admitted into the sanctuary of our lives influences that make for evil, we must break away from them at all costs. The sweeter and truer relationships of our life should arm us for the struggle, the prayers of a mother, the sorrow of true friends. This is the fear, countless times, in the hearts of the folks at home when their boy leaves them to win his way in the city, the deadly fear lest he should fall into evil habits, and into the clutches of evil men. They know that there are men whose touch, whose words, whose very look, is contamination. To give them entrance into our lives is to submit ourselves to the contagion of sin.

Friends should be chosen by a higher principle of selection than any worldly one, of pleasure, or usefulness, or by weak submission to the evil influences of our lot. They should be chosen for character, for goodness, for truth and trustworthiness, because they have sympathy with us in our best thoughts and holiest aspirations, because they have community of mind in the things of the soul. All other connections are fleeting and imperfect from the nature of the case. A relationship based on the physical withers when the first bloom fades: a relationship founded on the intellectual is only a little more secure, as it too is subject to caprice. All purely earthly partnerships, like all earthly treasures, are exposed to decay, the bite of the moth and the stain of the rust; and they must all have an end.

A young man may get opposing advice from two equally trusted counsellors. One will advise him to cultivate the friendship of the clever, because they will afterwards occupy places of power in the world: the other will advise him to cultivate the friendship of the good, because if they do not inherit the earth, they aspire to the heavens. If he knows the character of the two counsellors, he will understand why they should look upon life from such different standpoints; and later on he will find that while some of his friends were both clever and good, not one of the purely intellectual friendships remain to him. It does not afford a sufficient basis of agreement, to stand the tear and wear of life. The basis of friendship must be community of soul.

The only permanent severance of heart comes through lack of a common spiritual footing. If one soul goes up the mountain top, and the other stays down among the shadows, if the two have not the same high thoughts, and pure desires, and ideals of service, they cannot remain together except in form. Friends need not be identical in temperament and capacity, but they must be alike in sympathy. An unequal yoke becomes either an intolerable burden, or will drag one of the partners away from the path his soul at its best would have loved to tread.

If you loved only what were worth your love,
Love were clear gain, and wholly well for you. [13]

If we choose our friends in Christ, neither here, nor ever, need we fear parting, and will have the secure joy and peace which come from having a friend who is as one's own soul.

---

13 From "Among the rocks" in Robert Browning, *James Lee's Wife* (1834)

For Lycidas is dead, dead ere his prime.
Young Lycidas, and hath not left his peer.
. . . .
Weep no more, woeful shepherds, weep no more
For Lycidas, your sorrow, is not dead,
Sunk though he be beneath the watery floor,.
So sinks the day-star in the ocean bed,
And yet anon repairs his drooping head,
And tricks his beams, and with new-spangled ore
Flames in the forehead of the morning sky:
So Lycidas sunk low, but mounted high,
Through the dear might of him that walked the waves.
~ JOHN MILTON, *Lycidas*

Chapter 5

The Eclipse of Friendship

As it is one of the greatest joys of life when a kindred soul is for the first time recognized and claimed, so it is one of the bitterest moments of life when the first rupture is made of the ties which bind us to other lives. Before it comes, it is hard to believe that it is possible, if we ever think of it at all. When it does come, it is harder still to understand the meaning of the blow. The miracle of friendship seemed too fair, to carry in its bosom the menace of its loss. We knew, of course, that such things had been, and must be, but we never quite realized what it would be to be the victims of the common doom of man.

If it only came as a sudden pain, that passes after its brief spasm of agony, it would not be so sore an affliction; but when it comes, it comes to stay. There remains a place in our hearts which is tender to every touch, and it is touched so often. We survive the shock of the moment easier than the constant reminder of our loss. The old familiar face, debarred to the sense of sight, can be recalled by a stray word, a casual sight, a chance memory. The closer the intercourse had been, the more things there are in our lives associated with him—things that we did together, places that we visited together, thoughts even that we thought together.

There seems no region of life where we can escape from the suggestions of memory. The sight of any little object can bring him back, with his way of speaking, with his tricks of gesture, with all the qualities for which we loved him, and for which we mourn him now. If the intimacy was due to mere physical proximity, the loss will be only a vague sense of uneasiness through the breakdown of long-continued habit; but, if the two lives were woven into the same web, there must be ragged edges left, and it is a weary task to take up the threads again, and find a new woof for the warp. The closer the connection has been, the keener is the loss. It comes back to us at the sight of the many things associated with him, and, fill up our lives with countless distractions as we may, the shadow creeps back to darken the world.

Sometimes there is the added pain of remorse that we did not enough appreciate the treasure we possessed. In thoughtlessness we accepted the gift; we had so little idea of the true value of his friendship; we loved so little, and were so impatient: if only we had him back again; if only we had one more opportunity to show him how dear he was; if only we had another chance of proving ourselves worthy. We can hardly forgive ourselves that we were so cold and selfish. Self-reproach, the regret of the unaccepted opportunity, is one of the commonest feelings after bereavement, and it is one of the most blessed.

Still, it may become a morbid feeling. It is a false sentimentalism which lives in the past, and lavishes its tenderness on memory. It is difficult to say what is the dividing line between healthy sorrow and morbid sentiment. It seems a natural instinct, which makes the bereaved care lovingly for the very grave, and which makes the mother keep locked up the little shoes worn by the little feet, relics hid from the vulgar eye. The instinct has become a little more morbid, when it has preserved the room of a dead mother, with its petty decorations and ornaments as she left them. Beautiful as the instinct may be, there is nothing so dangerous as when our most natural feeling turns morbid.

It is always a temptation, which grows stronger the longer we live, to look back instead of forward, to bemoan the past, and thus deride the present and distrust the future. We must not forget our present blessings, the love we still possess, the gracious influences that remain, and most of all the duties that claim our strength. The loving women who went early in the morning to the sepulchre of the buried Christ were met with a rebuke, "Why seek ye the living among the dead?"[1] They were sent back to life to find him, and sent back to life to do honour to his death. Not by ointments and spices, however precious, nor at the rock-hewn tomb, could they best remember their Lord; but out in the world, which that morning had seemed so cold and cheerless, and in their lives, which then had seemed not worth living.

Christianity does not condemn any natural human feeling, but it will not let these interfere with present duty and destroy future usefulness. It does not send men to search for the purpose of living in the graves of their dead hopes and pleasures. Its disciples must not attempt to live on the relics of even great incidents, among crucifixes and tombs. In the desert, the heart must reach forward to the

---

1 Luke 24:5

Promised Land, and not back to Egypt. The Christian faith is for the future, because it believes in the God of the future. The world is not a lumber room, full of relics and remembrances, over which to brood. We are asked to remember the beautiful past which was ours, and the beautiful lives which we have lost, by making the present beautiful like it, and our lives beautiful like theirs. It is human to think that life has no future, if now it seems "full of griefs and graves." It comes like a shock to find that we must bury our sorrow, and come into contact with the hard world again, and live our common life once more. The Christian learns to do it, not because he has a short memory, but because he has a long faith. The voice of inspiration is heard oftener through the realities of life, than through vain regrets and recluse dreams. The Christian life must be in its degree something like the Master's own life, luminous with his hope, and surrounded by a bracing atmosphere which uplifts all who even touch its outer fringe.

The great fact of life, nevertheless, is death, and it must have a purpose to serve and a lesson to teach. It seems to lose something of its impressiveness, because it is universal. The very inevitableness of it seems to kill thought, rather than induce it. It is only when the blow strikes home, that we are pulled up and forced to face the fact. Theoretically there is a wonderful unanimity among men, regarding the shortness of life and the uncertainty of all human relationships. The last word of the wise on life has ever been its fleetingness, its appalling changes, its unexpected surprises. The only certainty of life is its uncertainty—its unstable tenure, its inevitable end. But practically we go on as if we could lay our plans, and mortgage time, without doubt or danger; until our feet are knocked from under us by some sudden shock, and we realize how unstable the equilibrium of life really is. The lesson of life is death.

The experience would not be so tragically universal, if it had not a good and necessary meaning. For one thing it should sober us, and make our lives full of serious, solemn purpose. It should "teach us to number our days, that we may apply our hearts to wisdom."[2] The man, who has no place for death in his philosophy has not learned to live. The lesson of death is life.

On the whole, however, it is not our own liability to death which oppresses us. The fear of it to a brave man, not to speak of a man of faith, can be overcome. It is the fear of it *for others* whom we love, which is its sting. And none of us can live very long without knowing in our own heart's experience the reality, as well as the terror, of death. This too has its meaning for us, to look at life more tenderly, and touch it more gently. The pathos of life is only a forced sentiment to us, if we have not felt the pity of life. To a sensitive soul, smarting with his own loss, the world sometimes seems full of graves, and for a time at least makes him walk softly among men.

This is one reason why the making of new friends is so much easier in youth than later on. Friendship comes to youth seemingly without any conditions, and without any fears. There is no past to look back at, with much regret and some sorrow. We never look behind us, *till we miss something.* Youth is satisfied with the joy of present possession. To the young friendship comes as the glory of spring, a very miracle of beauty, a mystery of birth: to the old it has the bloom of autumn, beautiful still, but with the beauty of decay. To the young it is chiefly hope: to the old it is mostly memory. The man who is conscious that he has lost the best of his days, the best of his powers, the best of his friends, naturally lives a good deal in the past.

Such a man is prepared for further losses; he has adjusted himself to the fact of death. At first, we cannot believe that it can happen to us and to our love; or, if the thought comes to us, it is an event too far in the future to ruffle the calm surface of our heart. And yet, it must come; from it none can escape. Most can remember a night of waiting, too stricken for prayer, too numb of heart even for feeling, vaguely expecting the blow to strike us out of the dark. A strange

---

2 Psalm 90:12

sense of the unreality of things came over us, when the black wave submerged us and passed on. We went out into the sunshine, and it seemed to mock us. We entered again among the busy ways of men, and the roar of life beat upon our brain and heart,

> *Yet in these ears, till hearing dies,*
> *One set slow bell will seem to toll,*
> *The passing of the sweetest soul*
> *That ever looked with human eyes.*[3]

Was it worthwhile to have linked our lives on to other lives, and laid ourselves open to such desolation? Would it not be better to go through the world, without joining ourselves too closely to the fleeting bonds of other loves? Why deliberately add to our disabilities? But it is not a disability; rather, the great purpose of all our living is to learn love, even though we must experience the pains of love as well as the joys. To cut ourselves off from this lot of the human would be to impoverish our lives, and deprive ourselves of the culture of the heart, which, if a man has not learned, he has learned nothing. Whatever the risks to our happiness, we cannot stand out from the lot of man, without ceasing to be men in the only true sense.

It is not easy to solve the problem of sorrow. Indeed there is no solution of it, unless the individual soul works out its own solution. Most attempts at a philosophy of sorrow just end in high-sounding words. Explanations, which profess to cover all the ground, are as futile as the ordinary blundering attempts at comfort, which only charm ache with sound and patch grief with proverbs. The sorrow of our hearts is not appreciably lessened by argument. Any kind of philosophy—any wordy explanation of the problem—is at the best poor comfort. It is not the problem which brings the pain in the first instance: it is the pain which brings the problem. The heart's bitterness is not allayed by an exposition of the doctrine of provi-

---

3 Alfred, Lord Tennyson, *In Memoriam* (1850)

dence. Rachel who weeps for her children, the father whose little daughter lies dead at home, are not to be appeased in their anguish by a nicely-balanced system of thought. Nor is surcease[4] of sorrow thus brought to the man to whom has come a bereavement, or a succession of bereavements, which makes him feel that all the glory and joy of life, its friendship and love and hope, have gone down into the grave, so that he can say,

Three dead men have I loved,
And thou wert last of the three.[5]

At the same time, if it be true that there is a meaning in friendship, a spiritual discipline to educate the heart and train the life, it must also be true that there is equally a meaning in the eclipse of friendship. If we have enough faith to see death to be good, we will find out for ourselves why it is good. It may teach us just what we were in danger of forgetting, some omission in our lives, which was making them shallow and poor. It may be to one a sight into the mystery of sin; to another a sight into the mystery of love. To one it comes with the lesson of patience, which is only a side of the lesson of faith; to another it brings the message of sympathy. As we turn the subject toward the light, there come gleams of colour from different facets of it.

All life is an argument for death. We cannot persist long in the effort to live the Christian life, without feeling the need for death. The higher the aims, and the truer the aspirations, the greater is the burden of living, until it would become intolerable. Sooner or later we are forced to make the confession of Job, "I would not live alway."[6] To live forever in this sordidness, to have no reprieve from the doom of sin, no truce from the struggle of sin, would be a fearful fate.

To the Christian, therefore, death cannot be looked on as evil; first,

---

4 Or cessation.

5 Alfred, Lord Tennyson, *In the Garden at Swainston* (1874)

6 Job 7:16

because it is universal, and it is universal because it is God-ordained. In St. Peter's, at Rome, there are many tombs, in which death is symbolized in its traditional form as a skeleton, with the fateful hour-glass and the fearful scythe. Death is the rude reaper, who cruelly cuts off life and all the joy of life. But there is one in which death is sculptured as a sweet gentle motherly woman, who takes her wearied child home to safer and surer keeping. It is a truer thought than the other. Death is a minister of God, doing his pleasure, and doing us good.

Again, it cannot be evil because it means a fuller life, and therefore an opportunity for fuller and further service. Faith will not let a man hasten the climax; for it is in the hands of love, as he himself is. But death is the climax of life. For if all life is an argument for death, then so also all death is an argument for life.

Jowett says,[7] in one of his letters, "I cannot sympathize in all the grounds of consolation that are sometimes offered on these melancholy occasions, but there are two things which have always seemed to me unchangeable: first, that the dead are in the hands of God, who can do for them more than we can ask or have; and secondly, with respect to ourselves, that such losses deepen our views of life, and make us feel that we would not always be here." These are two noble grounds of consolation, and they are enough.

Death is the great argument for immortality. We cannot believe that the living, loving soul has ceased to be. We cannot believe that all those treasures of mind and heart are squandered in empty air. We will not believe it. When once we understand the meaning of the spiritual, we see the absolute certainty of eternal life; we need no arguments for the persistence of being.

To appear for a little time and then vanish away, is the outward biography of all men, a circle of smoke that breaks, a bubble on the stream that bursts, a spark put out by a breath.

But there is another biography, a deeper and a permanent one, the biography of the soul. Everything that *appears* vanishes away:

---

7 Benjamin Jowett (1817-1893)

that is its fate, the fate of the everlasting hills as well as of the vapour that caps them. But that which does not appear, the spiritual and unseen, which we in our folly sometimes doubt because it does not appear, is the only reality; it is eternal and passeth not away. The material in nature is only the garb of the spiritual, as speech is the clothing of thought. With our vulgar standards we often think of the thought as the unsubstantial and the shadowy, and the speech as the real. But speech dies upon the passing wind; the thought alone remains. We consider the sound to be the music, whereas it is only the expression of the music, and vanishes away. Behind the material world, which waxes old as a garment, there is an eternal principle, the thought of God it represents. Above the sounds there is the music that can never die. Beneath our lives, which vanish away, there is a vital thing, spirit. We cannot locate it and put our finger on it; that is why it is permanent. The things we can put our finger on are the things which appear, and therefore which fade and die.

So, death to the spiritual mind is only *eclipse*. When there is an eclipse of the sun it does not mean that the sun is blotted out of the heavens: it only means that there is a temporary obstruction between it and us. If we wait a little, it passes. Love cannot die. Its forms may change, even its objects, but its life is the life of the universe. It is not death, but sleep: not loss, but eclipse. The love is only transfigured into something more ethereal and heavenly than ever before. Happy to have friends on earth, but happier to have friends in heaven.

And it need not be even eclipse, except in outward form. Communion with the unseen can mean true correspondence with all we have loved and lost, if only our souls were responsive. The highest love is not starved by the absence of its object; it rather becomes more tender and spiritual, with more of the ideal in it. Ordinary affection, on a lower plane, dependent on physical attraction, or on the earthly side of life, naturally crumbles to dust when its foundation is removed. But love is independent of time or space, and as a matter of fact is purified and intensified by absence. Separation of friends is not a physical thing. Lives can be sundered as if divided by infinite distance, even although materially they are near each other. This tragedy is often enough enacted in our midst.

The converse is also true; so that friendship does not really lose by death: it lays up treasure in heaven, and leaves the very earth a sacred place, made holy by happy memories. "The ruins of Time build mansions in Eternity," said William Blake, speaking of the death of a loved brother, with whose spirit he never ceased to converse. There are people in our homes and our streets whose highest life is with the dead. They live in another world. We can see in their eyes that their hearts are not here. It is as if they already saw the land that is very far off. It is only far off to our gross insensate senses.

The spiritual world is not outside this earth of ours. It includes it and pervades it, finding a new centre for a new circumference in every loving soul that has eyes to see the Kingdom. So, to hold commerce with the dead is not a mere figure of speech. Heaven lies about us not only in our infancy, but all our lives. We blind ourselves with dust, and in our blindness lay hold feverishly of the outside of life, mistaking the fugitive and evanescent for the truly permanent. If we only used our capacities we would take a more enlightened view of death. We would see it to be the entrance into a more radiant and a more abundant life not only for the friend that goes first, but for the other left behind.

Spiritual communion cannot possibly be interrupted by a physical change. It is because there is so little of the spiritual in our ordinary intercourse that death means silence and an end to communion. There is a picture of death, which, when looked at with the ordinary perspective, seems to be a hideous skull, but when seen near at hand is composed of flowers, with the eyes, in the seemingly empty sockets of the skull, formed by two fair faces of children. Death at a distance looks horrible, the ghastly spectre of the race; but with the near vision it is beautiful with youth and flowers, and when we look into its eyes we look into the stirrings of life.

Love is the only permanent relationship among men, and the permanence is not an accident of it, but is of its very essence. When released from the mere magnetism of sense, instead of ceasing to exist, it only then truly comes into its largest life. If our life were more a life in the spirit, we would be sure that death can be at the worst but the eclipse of friendship. Tennyson felt this truth in his own experience, and expressed it in noble form again and again in *In Memoriam*:

> *Sweet human hand and lips and eye,*
> *Dear heavenly friend that canst not die;*

> *Strange friend, past, present, and to be;*
> *Loved deeplier, darklier understood;*
> *Behold I dream a dream of good,*
> *And mingle all the world with thee.*

> *Thy voice is on the rolling air;*
> *I hear thee where the waters run;*
> *Thou standest in the rising sun,*
> *And in the setting thou art fair.*

It is not loss, but momentary eclipse, and the final issue is a clearer perception of immortal love, and a deeper consciousness of eternal life.

The attitude of mind, therefore, in any such bereavement—sore as the first stroke must be, since we are so much the creatures of habit, and it is hard to adjust ourselves to the new relationship—cannot be an attitude merely of resignation. That was the extent to which the imperfect revelation of the Old Testament brought men. They had to rest in their knowledge of God's faithfulness and goodness. The limit of their faith was, "The Lord gave, and the Lord hath taken away."[8] But to resignation we can add joy. "Not dead, but sleepeth,"[9] said the Master of death and life to a sorrowing man.

---

8 Job 1:21
9 Luke 8:52

For one thing it must mean the hallowing of memory. The eclipse of love makes the love fairer when the eclipse passes. The loss of the outward purifies the affection and softens the heart. It brings out into fact what was often only latent in feeling. Memory adds a tender glory to the past. We only think of the virtues of the dead: we forget their faults. This is as it should be. We rightly love the immortal part of them; the fire has burned up the dross and left pure gold. If it is idealization, it represents that which will be, and that which really is.

We do not ask to forget; we do not want the so-called consolations which time brings. Such an insult to the past, as forgetfulness would be, means that we have not risen to the possibilities of communion of spirit afforded us in the present. We would rather that the wound should be ever fresh than that the image of the dear past should fade. It would be a loss to our best life if it would fade. There is no sting in such a faith. Such remembrance as this, which keeps the heart green, will not cumber the life. True sentiment does not weaken, but becomes an inspiration to make our life worthy of our love. It can save even a squalid lot from sordidness; for however poor we may be in the world's goods, we are rich in happy associations in the past, and in sweet communion in the present, and in blessed hope for the future.

They parted—ne'er to meet again!
But never either found another
To free the hollow heart from paining—
They stood aloof, the scars remaining,
Like cliffs which had been rent asunder,
A dreary sea now rolls between;
But neither heat, nor frost, nor thunder,
Shall wholly do away, I ween,
The marks of that which once hath been.
~ SAMUEL TAYLOR COLERIDGE, *Christabel*

Chapter 6

The Wreck of Friendship

The eclipse of friendship through death is not nearly so sad as the many ways in which friendship may be wrecked. There are worse losses than the losses of death; and to bury a friendship is a keener grief than to bury a friend. The latter softens the heart and sweetens the life, while the former hardens and embitters. The Persian poet Hafiz says, "Thou learnest no secret until thou knowest friendship; since to the unsound no heavenly knowledge enters." But so imperfect are our human relationships, that many a man has felt that he has bought his knowledge too dearly. Few of us go through the world without some scars on the heart, which even yet throb if the finger of memory touch them. In spite of all that has been said, and may be said in praise of this golden friendship, it has been too often found how vain is the help of man. The deepest tragedies of life have been the failure of this very relationship.

In one way or other the loss of friendship comes to all. The shores of life are strewn with wrecks. The convoy which left the harbour gaily in the sunshine cannot all expect to arrive together in the haven. There are the danger of storms and collisions, the separation of the night, and even at the best, if accidents never occur, the whole company cannot all keep up with the speed of the swiftest.

There is a certain pathos in all loss, but there is not always pain in it, or at least it is of varied quality and extent. Some losses are natural and unavoidable, quite beyond our control, the result of resistless change. Some loss is even the necessary accompaniment of gain. The loss of youth with all its possessions is the gain of manhood and womanhood. A man must put away childish things, the speech and understanding and thought of a child. So the loss of some friendship comes as a part of the natural course of things, and is accepted without mutilating the life.

Many of our connections with people are admittedly casual and temporary. They exist for mutual convenience through common interest at the time, or common purpose, or common business. None of the partners asks for more than the advantage each derives from the connection. When it comes to an end, we let slip the cable easily, and say good-bye with a cheery wave. With many people we meet and part in all friendliness and good feeling, and will be glad to meet again, but the parting does not tear our affections by the roots. When the business is transacted the tie is loosed, and we each go our separate ways without much regret.

At other times there is no thought of gain, except the mutual advantage of conversation or companionship. We are pleasant to each other, and enjoy the intercourse of kindred tastes. Most of us have some pleasant recollections of happy meetings with interesting people, perhaps on holiday times, when we felt we would be glad to see them again if fortune turned round the wheel again to the same place; but, though hardly ever did it come about that an opportunity of meeting has occurred, we do not feel that our life is much the poorer for the loss.

Also, we *grow* out of some of our friendships. This is to be expected, since so many of them are formed thoughtlessly, or before we really knew either ourselves or our friends. They never meant very much to us. Most boyish friendships as a rule do not last long, because they are not based on the qualities which wear well. Schoolboy comradeships are usually due to propinquity[1] rather than to character. They are the fruit of accident rather than of affinity of soul. Boys grow out of these as they grow out of their clothes. Now and again they suffer from growing pains, but it is more discomfort than anything else.

It is sad to look back and realize how few of one's early companionships remain, but it is not possible to blame either party for the loss. Distance, separation of interest, difference of work, all operate to divide. When athletics seemed the end of existence, friendship was based on football and cricket. But as life opens out, other standards are set up, and a new principle of selection takes its place. When the world is seen to be more than a ball-ground, when it is recognized to be a stage on which men play many parts, a new sort of intimacy is demanded, and it does not follow that it will be with the same persons. Such loss as this is the condition which accompanies the gain of growth.

There is more chance for the permanence of friendships formed a little later. It must not be too long after this period, however; for, when the generous time of youth has wholly passed,

---

1 Or proximity.

it becomes hard to make new connections. Men get overburdened with cares and personal concerns, and grow cautious about making advances. In youth the heart is responsive and ready to be generous, and the hand aches for the grasp of a comrade's hand, and the mind demands fellowship in the great thoughts that are beginning to dawn upon it. The closest friendships are formed early in life, just because then we are less cautious, more open to impressions, and readier to welcome self-revelations. After middle life a man does not find it easy to give himself away, and keeps a firmer hand on his feelings. Whatever are the faults of youth, it is unworldly in its estimates as a rule, and uncalculating in its thoughts of the future.

The danger to such friendship is the danger of just letting it lapse. As life spreads out before the eager feet, new interests crop up, new relations are formed, and the old tie gets worn away, from want of adding fresh strands to it. We may believe the advice about not forsaking an old friend because the new is not comparable to him, but we can neglect it by merely letting things slip past, which if used would be a new bond of union.

As it is easier for some temperaments to make friends, it is easier for some dispositions to keep them. Little faults of manner, little occasions of thoughtlessness, or lack of the little courtesies, do more to separate people than glaring mistakes. There are some men so built that it is difficult to remain on very close terms with them, there are so many corners to knock against. Even strength of character, if unmodified by sweetness of disposition, adds to the difficulty of pulling together. Strong will can so easily develop into self-will; decision can become dogmatism; wit, the salt of conversation, loses its savour when it becomes ill-natured; a faculty for argument is in danger of being mere quarrelsomeness.

The ordinary amenities of life must be preserved among friends. We can never feel very safe with the man whose humour tends to bitter speaking or keen sarcasm, or with the man who flares up into hasty speech at every or no provocation, or with the man who is argumentative and assertive,

Who'd rather on a gibbet dangle
Than miss his dear delight, to wrangle.[2]

There are more breaches of the peace among friends through sins of speech, than from any other cause. We do not treat our friends with enough respect. We make the vulgar mistake of looking upon the common as if it were therefore cheap in nature. We ought rather to treat our friend with a sort of sacred familiarity, as if we appreciated the precious gift his friendship is.

Every change in a man's life brings a risk of letting go something of the past, which it is a loss to part with. A change of work, or a change of residence, or entrance into a larger sphere, brings a certain engrossment which leads to neglect of the richest intercourse in the past life. To many a man, even marriage has had a drop of bitterness in it, because it has somehow meant the severing of old and sacred links. This may be due to the vulgar reason of wives' quarrels, the result of petty jealousy; but it may be due also to preoccupation and a subtle form of selfishness. The fire needs to be kept alive with fuel. To preserve it, there must be forethought, and care, and love expended as before.

Friendship may lapse through the *misfortune of distance*. Absence does not always make the heart grow fonder. It only does so, when the heart is securely fixed, and when it is a heart worth fixing. More often the other proverb is truer, that it is out of sight out of mind. It is so easy for a man to become self-centred, and to impoverish his affections through sheer neglect. Ties once close get frayed and strained till they break, and we discover that we have said farewell to the past. Some kind of intercourse is needed to maintain friendship. There is a pathos about this gradual drifting away of lives, borne from each other, it sometimes seems, by opposing tides, as if a resistless power separated them,

---

2 Samuel Butler, *Hudibras*, Part III, Canto ii, "The Argument" (1664)

And bade betwixt their shores to be
The unplumbed, salt, estranging sea.[3]

Or friendship may lapse through the *fault of silence*. The misfortune of distance may be overcome by love, but the fault of silence crushes out feeling as the falling rain kills the kindling beacon. Even the estrangements and misunderstandings which will arise to all could not long remain, where there is a frank and candid interchange of thought. Hearts grow cold toward each other through neglect. There is a suggestive word from the old Scandinavian *Edda*, "Go often to the house of thy friend; for weeds soon choke up the unused path."[4] It is hard to overcome again the alienation caused by neglect; for there grows up a sense of resentment and injured feeling.

Among the petty things which wreck friendships none is so common and so unworthy as *money*. It is pitiable that it should be so. Thackeray speaks of the remarkable way in which a five-pound note will break up a half-century's attachment between two brethren, and it is a common cynical remark of the world that the way to lose a friend is to lend him money. [5]There is nothing which seems to affect the mind more, and colour the very heart's blood, than money. There seems a curse in it sometimes, so potent is it for mischief. Poverty, if it be too oppressive grinding down the face, may often hurt the heart-life; but perhaps oftener still it only reveals what true treasures there are in the wealth of the affections. Whereas, we know what heartburnings, and rivalries, and envyings, are occasioned by this golden apple of discord. Most of the disputes which separate brethren are about the dividing of the inheritance, and it does seem to be the case that few friendships can survive the test of money.

------

3 Matthew Arnold, *To Marguerite* (1852)
4 *Edda* is a thirteenth-century collection of Old Norse poems.
5 William Makepeace Thackeray, *Vanity Fair* (1847/1848)

Neither a borrower, nor a lender be;
For loan oft loses both itself and friend.[6]

There must be something wrong with the friendship which so breaks down. It ought to be able to stand a severer strain than that. But the inner reason of the failure is often that there has been a moral degeneracy going on, and a weakening of the fibre of character on one side, or on both sides. The particular dispute, whether it be about money or about anything else, is only the occasion which reveals the slackening of the morale. The innate delicacy and self-respect of the friend who asks the favour may have been damaged through a series of similar importunities, or there may have been a growing hardness of heart and selfishness in the friend who refuses the request. Otherwise, if two are on terms of communion, it is hard to see why the giving or receiving of this service should be any more unworthy than any other help, which friends can grant to each other. True commerce of the heart should make all other needful commerce possible. Communion includes communism. To have things in common does not seem difficult, when there is love in common.

Friendship has also been wrecked by *outside means,* by the evil of others, through the evil speaking, or the envy, or the whispering tongues that delight in scandal. Some mean natures rejoice in sowing discord, carrying tales with just the slightest turn of a phrase, or even a tone of the voice, which gives a sinister reading to an innocent word or act. Frankness can always prevent such from permanently wrecking friendship. Besides, we should judge no man, still less a trusted friend, by a report of an incident or a hasty word. We should judge our friend by his record, by what we know of his character. When anything inconsistent with that character comes before our notice, it is only justice to him to at least suspend judgment, and it would be wisdom to refuse to credit it at all.

We sometimes wonder to find a friend cold and distant to us, and

---

6 William Shakespeare, *Hamlet,* Act I, Scene iii

perhaps we moralize on the fickleness and inconstancy of men, but the reason may be to seek *in ourselves*. We cannot expect the pleasure of friendship without the duty, the privilege without the responsibility. We cannot break off the threads of the web, and then, when the mood is on us, continue it as though nothing had happened. If such a breakage has occurred, we must go back and patiently join the threads together again. Thoughtlessness has done more harm in this respect than ill-will. If we have lost a friend through selfish neglect, the loss is ours, and we cannot expect to take up the story where we left off years ago. There is a serene impudence about the treatment some mete out to their friends, dropping them whenever it suits, and thinking to take them up when it happens once more to suit. We cannot expect to walk with another, when we have gone for miles along another way. We will have to go back, and catch him up again. If the fault has been ours, desire and shame will give our feet wings.

The real source of separation is ultimately a *spiritual* one. We cannot walk with another unless we are agreed.[7] The lapse of friendship is often due to this, that one has let the other travel on alone. If one has sought pleasure, and the other has sought truth; if one has cumbered his life with the trivial and the petty, and the other has filled his with high thoughts and noble aspirations; if their hearts are on different levels, it is natural that they should now be apart. We cannot stay behind with the camp-followers, and at the same time fight in the van with the heroes. If we would keep our best friends, we must go with them in sympathy, and be able to share their thoughts. In the letters of Dean Stanley, there is one from Jowett to Stanley, which brings out this necessity.

I earnestly hope that the friendship, which commenced between us many years ago, may be a blessing to last us through life. I feel that if it is to be so we must both go onward, otherwise the tear and wear of life, and the "having travelled over each other's minds," and a thousand

---

7 Amos 3:3

*accidents will be sufficient to break it off. I have often felt the inability
to converse with you, but never for an instant the least alienation. There
is no one who would not think me happy in having such a friend.*

It is not, however, so much the equal pace of the mind which is
necessary, as the equal pace of the spirit. We may think about a very
brilliant friend that he will outstrip us, and outgrow us. The fear is
natural, but if there be spiritual oneness it is an unfounded fear.

*Yet oft, when sundown skirts the moor,
An inner trouble I behold,
A spectral doubt which makes me cold,
That I shall be thy mate no more.*[8]

But love is not dependent on intellect. The great bond of union is
not that both parties are alike in mind, but that they are *akin in soul*.
Mere intellect only divides men further than the ordinary natural and
artificial distinctions that already exist. There are endless instances of
this disuniting influence to be seen, in the contempt of learning for
ignorance, the derisive attitude which knowledge assumes toward
simplicity, the metropolitan disdain for provincial Galilee, the *rabies
theologica* which is ever ready to declare that this people that knoweth
not the law is accursed. It is love, not logic, which can unite men.
Love is the one solvent to break down all barriers, and love has
other grounds for its existence than merely intellectual ones. So that
although similarity of tastes is another bond and is perhaps necessary
for the perfect friendship, it is not its foundation; and if the foundation be not undermined, there is no reason why difference of
mental power should wreck the structure.

However it happens that friends are separated, it is always sad; for
the loss of a friendship is the loss of an ideal. Sadder than the pathos
of unmated hearts is the pathos of severed souls. It is always a pain

8 Alfred, Lord Tennyson, *In Memoriam* (1850)

to find a friend look on us with cold stranger's eyes, and to know ourselves dead to hopes of future intimacy. It is a pain even when we have nothing to blame ourselves with, much more so when we feel that ours is the fault. It would not seem to matter very much, if it were not such a loss to both; for friendship is one of the appointed means of saving the life from worldliness and selfishness. It is the greatest education in the world; for it is education of the whole man, of the affections as well as the intellect. Nothing of worldly success can make up for the want of it. And true friendship is also a moral preservative. It teaches something of the joy of service, and the beauty of sacrifice. We cannot live an utterly useless life, if we have to think for, and act for, another. It keeps love in the heart, and keeps God in the life.

The greatest and most irretrievable wreck of friendship is the result of a *moral breakdown* in one of the associates. Worse than the separation of the grave is the desolation of the heart by faithlessness. More impassable than the gulf of distance with the estranging sea, more separating than the gulf of death, is the great gulf fixed between souls through deceit and shame. It is as the sin of Judas. Said a sorrowful psalmist, who had known this experience, "Mine own familiar friend, in whom I trusted, which did eat of my bread, hath lifted up his heel against me."[9] And another psalmist sobs out the same lament, "It was not an enemy that reproached me, then I could have borne it… But it was thou, a man mine equal, my guide and mine acquaintance. We took sweet counsel together, and walked into the house of God in company."[10] The loss of a friend by any of the common means is not so hard, as to find a friend faithless. The trustful soul has often been disillusioned thus. The rod has broken in the hand that leant on it, and has left its red wound on the palm. There is a deeper wound on the heart.

The result of such a breakdown of comradeship is often bitterness,

---

9 Psalm 41:9
10 Psalm 55:12-14

and cynical distrust of man. It is this experience which gives point to the worldling's sneer, "Defend me from my friends, I can defend myself from my enemies." We cannot wonder sometimes at the cynicism. It is like treason within the camp, against which no man can guard. It is a stab in the back, a cowardly assassination of the heart. Treachery like this usually means a sudden fall from the ideal for the deceived one, and the ideal can only be recovered, if at all, by a slow and toilsome ascent, foot by foot and step by step.

Failure of one often leads to distrust of all. This is the terrible responsibility of friendship. We have more than the happiness of our friend in our power; we have his faith. Most men who are cynical about women are so, because of the inconstancy of one. Most sneers at friendship are, to begin with at least, the expression of individual pain, because the man has known the shock of the lifted heel. Distrust works havoc on the character; for it ends in unbelief of goodness itself. And distrust always meets with its own likeness, and is paid back in its own coin. Suspicion breeds suspicion, and the conduct of life on such principles becomes a tug-of-war in which Greek is matched with Greek.

The social virtues, which keep the whole community together, are thus closely allied to the supreme virtue of friendship. Aristotle had reason in making it the *nexus* between his ethics and his politics. Truth, good faith, honest dealing between man and man, are necessary for any kind of intercourse, even that of business. Men can do nothing with each other, if they have not a certain minimum of trust. There have been times when there seems to be almost an epidemic of faithlessness, when the social bond seems loosened, when men's hands are raised against each other, when confidence is paralyzed, and people hardly know whom to trust.

The prophet Micah, who lived in such a time, expresses this state of distrust: "Trust ye not any friend, put ye no confidence in a familiar friend... A man's enemies are of his own household."[11]

---

11 Micah 7:5-6

This means anarchy, and society becomes like a bundle of sticks with the cord cut. The cause is always a decay of religion; for law is based on morality, and morality finds its strongest sanction in religion. Selfishness results in anarchy, a reversion to the Ishmaelite type of life.

The story of the French Revolution has in it some of the darkest pages in the history of modern civilization, due to the breakdown of social trust. The Revolution, like Saturn, took to devouring her own children. Suspicion, during the reign of terror, brooded over the heads of men, and oppressed their hearts. The ties of blood and fellowship seemed broken, and the sad words of Christ had their horrid fulfillment, that the brother would deliver up the brother to death, and the father the child, and the children shall rise up against the parents and cause them to be put to death.[12] There are some awful possibilities in human nature. In Paris of these days a man had to be ever on his guard, to watch his acts, his words, even his looks. It meant for a time a collapse of the whole idea of the state. It was a panic, worse than avowed civil war. Friendship, of course, could have little place in such a frightful palsy of mutual confidence, though there were, for the honour of the race, some noble exceptions. The wreck of friendship through deceit is always a step toward social anarchy; for it helps to break down trust and good faith among men.

The wreck of friendship is also a blow to religion. Many have lost their faith in God, because they have lost, through faithlessness, their faith in man. Doubt of the reality of love becomes doubt of the reality of the spiritual life. To be unable to see the divine in man, is to have the eyes blinded to the divine anywhere. Deception in the sphere of love shakes the foundation of religion. Its result is atheism, not perhaps as a conscious speculative system of thought, but as a subtle practical influence on conduct. It corrupts the fountain of life, and taints the whole stream. Despair of love, if final and complete, would be despair of God; for God is love. Thus, the wreck of friendship

---

12 Matthew 10:21

often means a temporary wreck of faith. It ought not to be so; but that there is a danger of it should impress us with a deeper sense of the responsibility attached to our friendships. Our life follows the fortunes of our love.

Perhaps we may go further, and say that friends, whose friendship has been broken off, should not entirely forget their former intercourse; and that just as we hold that we ought to serve friends before strangers, so former friends have some claims upon us on the ground of past friendship, unless extraordinary depravity were the cause of our parting.
~ ARISTOTLE, *Nicomachean Ethics*

Chapter 7

The Renewing of Friendship

I t is a sentiment of the poets and romancers that love is rather helped by quarrels. There must be some truth in it, as we find the idea expressed a hundred times in different forms in literature. We find it among the wisdom of the ancients, and it remains still as one of the conventional properties of the dramatist, and one of the accepted traditions of the novelist. It is expressed in maxim and apothegm,[1] in play and poem. One of our old pre-Elizabethan writers has put it in classic form in English:

The falling out of faithful friends, renewing is of love.[2]

It is the chief stock-in-trade of the writer of fiction, to depict the misunderstandings which arise between two persons, through the sin of one, or the folly of both, or the villainy of a third; then come the means by which the tangled skein is unravelled, and in the end everything is satisfactorily explained, and the sorely-tried characters are ushered into a happiness stronger and sweeter than ever before. Friends quarrel, and are miserable in their state of separation; and afterward, when the friendship is renewed, it is discovered that the bitter dispute was only a blessing in disguise, as the renewal itself was an exquisite pleasure, and the result has been a firmer and more stable relationship of love and trust.

The truth in this sentiment is, of course, the evident one, that a man often only wakens to the value of a possession when he is in danger of losing it. The force of a current is sometimes only noted when it is opposed by an obstacle. Two persons may discover, by a temporary alienation, how much they really care for each other. It may be that previously they took things for granted. Their affection had lost its first glitter, and was accepted as commonplace. Through some misunderstanding or dispute, they broke off their friendly relationship, feeling sure that they had come to an end of their regard. They could never again be on the same close terms; hot words had been spoken; taunts and reproaches had passed; eyes had flashed fire, and they parted in anger—only to learn that their love for each other was as real and as strong as ever. The very difference revealed the true union of hearts that had existed. They had been blind to the strength of their mutual regard, till it was so painfully brought

1 Or pithy saying.

2 Richard Edwardes, *Amantium Irae* (c.1570s)

to their notice. The love is renewed with a more tender sense of its sacredness, and a more profound feeling of its strength. The dissensions only displayed the union; the discord drove them to a fuller harmony. This is a natural and common experience.

But a mistake may easily be made by confusing cause and effect. "The course of true love never did run smooth"[3]—but the obstacles in the channel do not *produce* the swiftness and the volume of the stream; they only *show* them. There may be an unsuspected depth and force for the first time brought to light when the stream strikes a barrier, but the barrier is merely the occasion, not the cause, of the revelation. To mistake the one for the other, may lead to a false and stupid policy. Many, through this mistake, act as though dissension were of the very nature of affection, and as if the one must necessarily react on the other for good. Some foolish people will sometimes even produce disagreement for the supposed pleasure of agreeing once more, and quarrel for the sake of making it up again.

Rather, the end of love is near at hand, when wrangling can live in its presence. It is not true that love is helped by quarrels, except in the small sense already indicated. A man may quarrel once too often with his friend, and a brother offended, says the proverb, is harder to be won than a strong city, and such contentions are like the bars of a castle.[4] It is always a dangerous experiment to willfully test affection, besides being often a cruel one. Disputing is a shock to confidence, and without confidence friendship cannot continue. A state of feud, even though a temporary one, often embitters the life, and leaves its mark on the heart. Desolated homes and lonely lives are witnesses of the folly of any such policy. From the root of bitterness there cannot possibly blossom any of the fair flowers of love. The surface truth of the poets' sentiment we have acknowledged and accounted for, but it is only a surface truth. The best of friends will fall out, and the best of them will renew their friendship, but it

---

3 William Shakespeare, *A Midsummer Night's Dream*, Act I, Scene i
4 Proverbs 18:19

is always at a great risk, and sometimes it strains the foundations of their esteem for each other to shaking:

And blessings on the falling out
That all the more endears,
When we fall out with those we love
And kiss again with tears![5]

But in any serious rupture of friendship it can be only a blessing when it means the tears of repentance, and these are often tears of blood. In all renewing there must be an element of repentance, and however great the joy of having regained the old footing, there is the memory of pain, and the presence of regret. To cultivate contention as an art, and to trade upon the supposed benefit of renewing friendship, is a folly which brings its own retribution.

The disputatious person for this reason never makes a good friend. In friendship men look for peace, and concord, and some measure of content. There are enough battles to fight outside, enough jarring and jostling in the street, enough disputing in the marketplace, enough discord in the workaday world, without having to look for contention in the realm of the inner life also. There, if anywhere, we ask for an end to strife. Friendship is the sanctuary of the heart, and the peace of the sanctuary should brood over it. Its chiefest glory is that the dust and noise of contest are excluded.

It must needs be that offences come. It is not only that the world is full of conflict and controversy, and every man must take his share in the fights of his time. We are born into the battle; we are born for the battle. But apart from the outside strife, from which we cannot separate ourselves, and do not desire to separate ourselves if we are true men, the strange thing is that it looks as if it must needs be that offences come even among brethren. The bitterest disputes in life are among those who are nearest each other in spirit. We do not quarrel

---

5 Alfred Lord Tennyson, *The Princess* (1847)

with the man in the street, the man with whom we have little or no communication. He has not the chance, nor the power, to chafe our soul, and ruffle our temper. If need be, we can afford to despise, or at least to neglect him. It is the man of our own household, near us in life and spirit, who runs the risk of the only serious dissensions with us. The man with whom we have most points of contact presents the greatest number of places where difference can occur. Only from circles that touch each other can a tangent strike off from the same point. A man can only make enemies among his friends. A certain amount of opposition and enmity a man must be prepared for in this world, unless he live a very invertebrate life. Outside opposition cannot embitter, for it cannot touch the soul. But that two who have walked as friends, one in aim and one in heart, perhaps of the same household of faith, should stand face to face with hard brows and gleaming eyes, should speak as foes and not as lovers of the same love, is, in spite of the poets and romancers, the bitterest moment of life.

There are some we cannot hurt even if we would; whom all the venom of our nature could not touch, because we mean nothing to them. But there are others in our power, whom we can stab with a word, and these are our brethren, our familiar friends, our comrades at work, our close associates, our fellow labourers in God's vineyard. It is not the crowd that idly jostle us in the street who can hurt us to the quick, but a familiar friend in whom we trusted. He has a means of ingress barred to strangers, and can strike home as no other can. This explains why family quarrels, ruptures in the inner circle, church disputes, are so bitter. They come so near us. An offended brother is hard to win, because the very closeness of the previous intimacy brings a rankling sense of injustice and the resentment of injured love. An injury from the hand of a friend seems such a wanton thing, and the heart hardens itself with the sense of wrong, and a separation ensues like the bars of a castle.

It must needs be that offences come, but woe unto him by whom they come. The strife-makers find in themselves, in their barren heart and empty life, their own appropriate curse. The blow they strike comes back upon themselves. Worse than the choleric temperament is the peevish, sullen nature. The one usually finds a speedy repentance for his hot and hasty mood; the other is a constant menace to friendship, and acts like a perpetual irritant. Its root is selfishness, and it grows by what it feeds on.

When offences do come, we may indeed use them as opportunities for growth in gracious ways, and thus turn them into blessings on the lives of both. To the offended it may be an occasion for patience and forgiveness; to the offender, an occasion for humility and frank confession; and to both, a renewing of love less open to offence in the future. There are some general counsels about the making up of differences, though each case needs special treatment for itself, which will easily be found if once the desire for concord be established. Christ's recipe for a quarrel among brethren is: "If thy brother shall trespass against thee, go and tell him his fault between thee and him alone: if he shall hear thee, thou hast gained thy brother."[6]

Much of our dissension is due to misunderstanding, which could be put right by a few honest words and a little open dealing. Human beings so often live at cross purposes with each other, when a frank word, or a simple confession of wrong, almost a look or a gesture, would heal the division. Resentment grows through brooding over a fancied slight. Hearts harden themselves in silence, and, as time goes on, it becomes more difficult to break through the silence. Often there are strained relations among men, who, at the bottom of their hearts, have sincere respect for each other, and smouldering affection also, which only needs a little coaxing of the spark to burst out again into a dancing flame. There is a terrible waste of human friendship, a waste of power which might be used to bless all our lives, through our sinful separations, our selfish exclusiveness, our resentful pride. We let the sweetest souls we have met die without acknowledging our debt to them. We stand aside in haughty isolation,

6 Matthew 18:15

till the open grave opens our sealed hearts—too late. We let the chance of reconciliation pass till it is irrevocable. Most can remember a tender spot in the past somewhere, a sore place, a time when discord entered with another they loved, and

Each spake words of high disdain
And insult to his heart's best brother.[7]

And in some cases, as with the friends in Coleridge's great poem, the parting has been eternal, and neither has ever since found another such friend to fill the life with comfort, and free the hollow heart from paining.

There is more evil from such a state of discord than the mere loss it is to both; it influences the whole heart-life, creating sometimes bitterness, sometimes universal suspicion, sometimes cynicism. Hatred is contagious, as love is. They have an effect on the whole character, and are not confined to the single incident which causes the love or the hate. To hate a single one of God's creatures is to harden the heart to some extent against all. Love is the centre of a circle, which broadens out in ever-widening circumference. Dante tells us in *La Vita Nuova* that the effect of his love for Beatrice was to open his heart to all, and to sweeten all his life. He speaks of the surpassing virtue of her very salutation to him in the street.

When she appeared in any place, it seemed to me, by the hope of
her excellent salutation, that there was no man mine enemy any longer;
and such warmth of charity came upon me that most certainly in that
moment I would have pardoned whomsoever had done me an injury;
and if any one should then have questioned me concerning any matter,
I could only have said unto him "Love," with a countenance clothed
in humbleness.[8]

---

7 Samuel Taylor Coleridge, *Christabel* (1797)
8 Dante Alighieri, *The New Life* (1293)

His love bred sweetness in his mind, and took in everything within the blessed sweep of its range. Hatred also is the centre of a circle, which has a baneful effect on the whole life. We cannot have bitterness or resentment in our mind without its colouring every thought and affection. Hate of one will affect our attitude toward all.

If, then, we possess the spirit to be reconciled with an offended or an offending brother, there are some things which may be said about the tactics of renewing the broken tie. There is needed a certain tactful considerateness. In all such questions the grace of the act depends as much on the *manner* of it, as on the act itself. The grace of the fairest act may be hurt by a boorish blemish of manner. Many a graceful act is spoiled by a graceless touch, as a generous deed can be ruined by a grudging manner. An air of condescension will destroy the value of the finest charity. There is a forgiveness which is no forgiveness—formal, constrained, from the teeth and lips outward. It does not come as the warm breath which has had contact with the blood of the heart. The highest forgiveness is so full and free, that it is forgetfulness. It is complete as the forgiveness of God.

If there is something in the method of the approach, there is perhaps more in the *time* of it. It ought to be chosen carefully and considerately; for it may be that the other has not been prepared for the renewal by thought and feeling, as the man who makes the advances has been. No hard and fast rule can be formulated when dealing with such a complex and varied subject as man. So much depends on temper and character. One man taken by surprise reveals his true feeling; another, when taken off his guard, is irritated, and shuts up his heart in a sort of instinctive self-defence. The thoughtfulness of love will suggest the appropriate means, but some emphasis may rightly be given to the phrase in Christ's counsel, "between thee and him alone." Let there be an opportunity for a frank and private conversation. To appeal to an estranged friend before witnesses induces to special pleading, making the witnesses the jury, asking for a verdict on either side; and the result is that both are still convinced they have right on their side, and that they have been wronged.

If the fault of the estrangement lies with us, the burden of confession should rest upon us also. To go to him with sincere penitence is no more than our duty. Whether the result be successful or not, it will mean a blessing for our own soul. Humility brings its own reward; for it brings God into the life. Even if we have cause to suspect that the offended brother will not receive us kindly, still such reparation as we can make is at least the gate to reconciliation. It may be too late, but confession will lighten the burden on our own heart. Our brother may be so offended that he is harder to be won than a strong city, but he is far more worth winning; and even if the effort be unsuccessful, it is better than the cowardice which suffers a bloodless defeat.

If, on the other hand, the fault was not ours, our duty is still clear. It should be even easier to take the initiative in such a case; for after all it is much easier to forgive than to submit to be forgiven. To some natures it is hard to be laid under an obligation, and the generosity of love must be shown by the offended brother. He must show the other his fault gently and generously, not parading his forgiveness like a virtue, but as if the favour were on his side—as it is. Christ made forgiveness the test of spirituality. If we do not know the grace of forgiveness, we do not know how gracious life may be. The highest happiness is not a matter of possessions and material gains, but has its source in a heart at peace; and thus it is that the renewing of friendship has a spiritual result. If we are revengeful, censorious, judging others harshly, always putting the worst construction on a word or an act, uncharitable, unforgiving, we certainly cannot claim kinship with the spirit of the Lord Jesus. St. Paul made the opposite the very test of the spiritual man: "Brethren, if a man be overtaken in a fault, ye which are spiritual, restore such an one in the spirit of meekness."[9]

If we knew all, we would forgive all. If we knew all the facts, the things which produced the petulance, the soreness which caused

---

9 Galatians 6:1

the irritation, we would be ready to pardon; for we would understand the temptation. If we knew all, our hearts would be full of
pitiful love even for those who have wronged us. They have
wronged themselves more than they can possibly wrong us; they
have wounded a man to their own hurt. To think kindly once more
of a separated friend, to soften the heart toward an offending
brother, will bring the blessing of the Peacemaker, the blessing of
the Reconciler. The way to be sure of acting this part is to pray for
him. We cannot remain angry with another, when we pray for him.
Offence departs, when prayer comes. The captivity of Job was turned,
when he prayed for his friends.

If we stubbornly refuse the renewing of friendship, it is an offence
against religion also. Only love can fulfil the law of Christ. His is the
gospel of reconciliation, and the greater reconciliation includes the
lesser. The friends of Christ must be friends of one another. That
ought to be accepted as an axiom. To be reconciled to God carries
with it at least a disposition of heart, which makes it easy to be
reconciled to men also. We have cause to suspect our religion, if it
does not make us gentle, and forbearing, and forgiving; if the love of
our Lord does not so flood our hearts as to cleanse them of all bitterness, and spite, and wrath. If a man is nursing anger, if he is letting
his mind become a nest of foul passions, malice, and hatred, and evil
wishing, how dwelleth the love of God in him?

If we cannot, at need, even humiliate ourselves to win our
brother, it is difficult to see where our religion comes in, especially
when we think what humiliation Christ suffered, that he might
reconcile us to God, and make us friends again with our heavenly
Father, and renew our broken love. Whatever be our faith and
works, and however correct be our creed and conduct, if we are
giving place to anger, if we are stiffening ourselves in strife and
disdain, we are none of his, who was meek and lowly of heart. We
may come to the sanctuary with lips full of praises and eyes full of
prayers, with devotion in our hearts and gifts in our hand, but God
will spurn our worship and despise our gifts. It is not a small matter,

this renewing of friendship, but is the root of religion itself, and is well made the very test of spiritual-mindedness. "If thou bring thy gift to the altar, and there rememberest that thy brother hath aught against thee; leave there thy gift before the altar, and go thy way; first be reconciled to thy brother, and then come and offer thy gift."[10] Misunderstandings and estrangements will arise, occasions will come when it seems as if not even love and forbearance can avoid a quarrel, but surely Christ has died in vain if his grace cannot save us from the continuance of strife.

Such renewing of love, done with this high motive, will indeed bring an added joy, as the poets have declared. The very pain will give zest to the pleasure. We will take the great gift of friendship with a new sense of its beauty and sacredness. We will walk more softly because of the experience, and more than ever will tremble lest we lose it. For days after the reconciliation, we will go about with the feeling that the benediction of the peacemakers[11] rests on our head and clings round our feet.

But more than any personal joy from the renewed friendship, we will have the smile of God on our life. We will know that we have done what is well pleasing in his sight. Sweeter than the peace which comes from being at one with men, is the peace which comes from being at one with God. It settles on the soul like the mist on the mountains, enveloping and enswathing it. It comes to our fevered life as a great calm. Over the broken waters there hovers the golden glory of God's eternal peace.

And more even than all that, we will have gained a new insight into the love of the Father, and into the sacrifice of the Son. We will understand a little more of the mystery of the Love which became poor, which gladly went into the wilderness to seek and to save the lost. The cross will gain new and rich significance to us, and all the world will be an arena in which is enacted the spectacle of God's

---

10 Matthew 5:23-24
11 Matthew 5:9

great love. The world is bathed in the love of God, as it is flooded by the blessed sun. If we are in the light and walk in love, our walk will be with God, and his gentleness will make us great. There is intended an ever fuller education in the meaning, and in the life of love, until the assurance reaches us that nothing can separate us from love.[12] Even death, which sunders us from our friends, cannot permanently divide us. In the great homecoming and reunion of hearts, all the veils which obscure feeling will be torn down, and we shall know each other better, and shall love each other better.

But every opportunity carries a penalty; every privilege brings with it a warning. If we will not live the life of love, if we harden our heart against a brother offended, we will find in our need even the great and infinite love of God shut against us, harder to be won than a strong city, ribbed and stockaded as the bars of a castle. To the unforgiving there is no forgiveness. To the hard, and relentless, and loveless, there is no love. To the selfish, there is no heaven.

---

12 Romans 8:38-39

If thy brother, the son of thy mother, or thy son, or thy daughter, or the wife of thy bosom, or thy friend which is as thine own soul, entice thee secretly, saying, Let us go and serve other gods... Thou shalt not consent unto him, nor hearken unto him... but thine hand shall be first upon him to put him to death, and afterwards the hand of all the people; ...because he has sought to thrust thee away from the Lord thy God.
~ DEUTERONOMY 13:6–10

Yet each will have one anguish—his own soul, Which perishes of cold.
~ MATTHEW ARNOLD, *Progress*

Chapter 8

The Limits of Friendship

F riendship, at its very best and purest, has limits. At its beginning, it seems to have no conditions, and to be capable of endless development. In the first flush of newborn love it seems almost an insult to question its absolute power to meet every demand made upon it. The exquisite joy of understanding, and being understood, is too keen to let us believe that there may be a terminal line beyond which we may not pass. Friendship comes

99

as a mystery, formless, undefined, without set bounds; and it is often
a sore experience to discover that it is circumscribed, and limited
like everything human. At first to speak of it as having qualifications
was a profanation, and to find them out came as a disillusionment.

Yet the discovery is not all a loss. The limitless is also the vague,
and it is well to know the exact terms implied in a relationship. Of
course we learn through experience the restrictions on all intimacy,
and if we are wise we learn to keep well within the margin; but many
a disappointment might have been saved, if we had understood the
inherent limitations of the subject. These are the result of personality.
Each partner is after all a distinct individual, with will, and conscience,
and life apart, with a personal responsibility which none can take
from him, and with an individual bias of mind and heart which can
never be left out of account.

As is to be expected, some of the limits of friendship are not
essential to the relation, but are due to a *defect* in the relation, perhaps
an idiosyncrasy of character or a peculiarity of temper. Some of
the limits are self-imposed, and arise from mistake or folly. A friend
may be too exacting, and may make excessive demands, which
strain the bond to the breaking point. There is often a good deal
of selfishness in the affection, which asks for absorption, and is
jealous of other interests. Jealousy is usually the fruit, not of love,
but of self-love. Life is bigger than any relationship, and covers more
ground. The circles of life may intersect, and part of each be common to the other, but there will be an area on both sides exclusive
to each; and even if it were possible for the circles to be concentric,
it could hardly be that the circumference of the two could be the
same; one would be, almost without a doubt, of larger radius than
the other. It is not identity which is the aim and the glory of
friendship, but unity in the midst of difference. To strive at identity
is to be certain of failure, and it deserves failure; for it is the outcome of selfishness. A man's friend is not his property, to be claimed
as his exclusive possession. Jealousy is an ignoble vice, because it
has its roots in egotism. It also destroys affection, since it is an

evidence of want of trust, and trust is essential to friendship.

There are physical limits to friendship, if nothing else. There are material barriers to be surmounted, before human beings really get into touch with each other, even in the slightest degree. The bodily organs, through which alone we can enter into communication, carry with them their own disabilities. The senses are at the best limited in their range, and are ever exposed to error. Flesh stands in the way of a complete revelation of soul. Human feet cannot enter past the threshold of the soul's abode. The very means of self-revelation is a self-concealment. The medium, by which alone we know, darkens, if it does not distort, the object. Words obscure thought, by the very process through which alone thought is possible for us; and the fleshly wrappings of the soul hide it, at the same time that they make it visible.

And if there are physical limits to friendship, there are greater mental limits. The needs of living press on us, and drive us into different currents of action. Our varied experience colours all our thought, and gives a special bias to our mind. There is a personal equation which must always be taken into account. This is the charm of intercourse, but it is also a limitation. We do not travel over the same ground; we meet, but we also part. However great the sympathy, it is not possible completely to enter into another man's mind, and look at a subject with his eyes. Much of our impatience with each other, and most of our misunderstandings, are caused by this natural limitation. The lines along which our minds travel can at the best be asymptotic, approaching each other indefinitely near, but never quite coinciding.

The greatest limit of friendship, of which these other are but indications, is the spiritual fact of the separate personality of each human being. This is seen most absolutely in the sphere of morals. The ultimate standard for a man is his own individual conscience, and neither the constraint of affection, nor the authority of numbers, can atone for falseness there. One of the most forceful illustrations of this final position of all religion is to be found in the passage of terrific intensity from the Book of Deuteronomy, which we have transcribed as a preface to this chapter. The form of the passage of course gets its colouring from the needs of the time and the temper of the age. The Book of Deuteronomy is so sure that the law of God is necessary for the life of Israel, and that departure from it will mean national ruin, that it will shrink from nothing needed to preserve the truth. Its warnings against being led away to idolatry are very instant and solemn. Every precaution must be taken; nothing must be allowed to seduce them from their allegiance, not the most sacred ties, nor the most solemn authority. No measure of repression can be too stern. In that fierce time it was natural that apostasy should be thought worthy of death; for apostasy from religion meant also treason to the nation: much more those who used their influence to seduce men to apostasy were to be condemned. The passage is introduced by the assertion that if even a prophet, a recognized servant of God, attesting his prophecy with signs and wonders, should solicit them to leave the worship of Jehovah, in spite of his sacred character, and in spite of the seeming evidence of miracles, they must turn from him with loathing, and his doom should be death. And if the apostasy should have the weight of numbers and a whole city go astray, the same doom is theirs. If the tenderest relationship should tempt the soul away, if a brother, or son, or daughter, or wife, or friend, should entice to apostasy, the same relentless judgment must be meted out.

The fact that this stern treatment is advocated in this book, which is full of the most tender consideration for all weak things, shows the need of the time. Deuteronomy has some of the most beautiful legislation in favour of slaves and little children and birds and domestic animals, some of it in advance of even our modern customs and practices, permeated as these are by Christian sentiment. And it is in this finely sensitive book that we find such strong assertion of the paramount importance of individual responsibility.

The influence of a friend or near relative is bound to be great. We are affected on every side, and at every moment, by the environment of other lives. There is a spiritual affinity, which is the closest and most powerful thing in the world, and yet in the realm of morals it has definite limits set to it. At the best it can only go a certain length, and ought not to be allowed to go further than its legitimate bounds. The writer of Deuteronomy appreciated to the full the power and attraction of the near human relationships. We see this from the way he describes them, adding an additional touch of fondness to each, "thy brother, the son of thy mother...or the wife of thy bosom...or thy friend, which is as thine own soul."[1] But it sets a limit to the place even such tender ties should be allowed to have. The most intimate of relatives, the most trusted of friends, must not be permitted to abrogate the place of conscience. Affection may be perverted into an instrument of evil. There is a higher moral law than even the law of friendship. The demands of friendship must not be allowed to interfere with the dictates of duty. It is not that the moral law should be blindly obeyed, but because in obeying it we are choosing the better part for both; for as Frederick Robertson truly says, "the man who prefers his dearest friend to the call of duty, will soon show that he prefers himself to his dearest friend." Such weak giving in to the supposed higher demand of friendship is only a form of selfishness.

Friendship is sometimes too exacting. It asks for too much, more than we have to give, more than we ever ought to give. There is a tyranny of love, making demands which can only be granted to the loss of both. Such tyranny is a perversion of the nature of love, which is to serve, not to rule. It would override conscience, and break down the will. We cannot give up our personal duty, as we cannot give up our personal responsibility. That is how it is possible for Christ to say that if a man love father, or mother, or wife more than him, he is not worthy of him.[2] No human being can take the place of God to another life; it is an acted blasphemy to attempt it.

There is a love which is evil in its selfishness. Its very exclusive

---

1 Deuteronomy 13:6
2 Matthew 10:37

claim is a sign of its evil root. The rights of the individual must not be renounced, even for love's sake. Human love can ask too much, and it asks too much when it would break down the individual will and conscience.

> *The hands that love us often are the hands*
> *That softly close our eyes and draw us earthward.*
> *We give them all the largesse of our life—*
> *Not this, not all the world, contenteth them,*
> *Till we renounce our rights as living souls.*

We cannot renounce our rights as living souls without losing our souls. No man can pay the debt of life for us. No man can take the burden of life from us. To no man can we hand over the reins unreservedly. It would be cowardice, and cowardice is sin. The first axiom of the spiritual life is the sacredness of the individuality of each. We must respect each other's personality. Even when we have rights over other people, these rights are strictly limited, and carry with them a corresponding duty to respect their rights also. The one intolerable despotism in the world is the attempt to put a yoke on the souls of men, and there are some forms of intimacy which approach that despotism. To transgress the moral bounds set to friendship is to make the highest forms of friendship impossible; for these are only reached when free spirits meet in the unity of the spirit.

The community of human life, of which we are learning much today, is a great fact. We are all bound up in the same bundle. In a very true sense we stand or fall together. We are ever on our trial as a society; not only materially, but even in the highest things morally and spiritually. There is a social conscience, which we affect, and which constantly affects us. We cannot rise very much above it; to fall much below it, is for all true purposes to cease to live. We have recognized social standards which test morality; we have common ties, common duties, common responsibilities.

But with it all, in spite of the fact of the community of human life, there is the other fact of the singleness of human life. We have a life, which we must live *alone*. We can never get past the ultimate fact of the personal responsibility of each. We may be leaves from the same tree of life, but no two leaves are alike. We may be wrapped up in the same bundle, but one bundle can contain very different things. Each of us is coloured with his own shade, separate and peculiar. We have our own special powers of intellect, our own special experience, our own moral conscience, our own moral life to live. So, while it is true that we stand or fall together, it is also true—and it is a deeper truth—that we stand or fall alone.

In this crowded world, with its intercourse and jostling, with its network of relationships, with its mingled web of life, we are each alone. Below the surface there is a deep, and below the deep there is a deeper depth. In the depth of the human heart there is, and there must be, solitude. There is a limit to the possible communion with another. We never completely open up our nature to even our nearest and dearest. In spite of ourselves something is kept back. Not that we are untrue in this, and hide our inner self, but simply that we are unable to reveal ourselves entirely. There is a bitterness of the heart which only the heart knoweth; there is a joy of the heart with which no stranger can intermeddle; there is a bound beyond which even a friend who is as our own soul becomes a stranger. There is a Holy of Holies, over the threshold of which no human feet can pass. It is safe from trespass, guarded from intrusion, and even we cannot give to another the magic key to open the door. In spite of all the complexity of our social life, and the endless connections we form with others, there is as the ultimate fact a great and almost weird solitude. We may fill up our hearts with human fellowship in all its grades, yet there remains to each a distinct and separated life.

We speak vaguely of the mass of men, but the mass consists of units, each with his own life, a thing apart. The community of human life is being emphasized today, and it is a lesson which bears and needs repetition, the lesson of our common ties and common duties. But at the same time we dare not lose sight of the fact of the singleness of human life, if for no other reason than that, otherwise we have no moral appeal to make on behalf of those ties and duties. In the region of morals, in dealing with sin, we see how true this solitude is. There may be what we can truly call social and national sins, and men can sin together, but in its ultimate issue sin is individual. It is a disintegrating thing, separating a man from his fellows, and separating him from God. We are alone with our sin, like the Ancient Mariner with the bodies of his messmates around him, each cursing him with his eye.[3] In the last issue, there is nothing in the universe but God and the single human soul. Men can share the sinning with us; no man can share the sin. "And the sin ye do by two and two ye must pay for one by one."[4] Therefore in this sphere of morals there must be limits to friendship, even with the friend who is as our own soul.

Friendship is a very real and close thing. It is one of the greatest joys in life, and has noble fruits. We can do much for each other: there are burdens we can share: we can rejoice with those who do rejoice, and weep with those who weep.[5] Through sympathy and love we are able to get out of self; and yet even here there are limits. Our helplessness in the presence of grief proves this fundamental singleness of human life. When we stand beside a friend before the open grave, under the cloud of a great sorrow, we learn how little we can do for him. We can only stand speechless, and pray that the great Comforter may come with his own divine tenderness, and enter the sanctuary of sorrow shut to feet of flesh. Mourners have indeed been soothed by a touch, or a look, or a prayer, which had their source in a pitiful human heart, but it is only as a message of condolence flashed from one world to another. There is a burden which every man must bear, and none can bear for him; for there is

---

3 Samuel Taylor Coleridge, *The Rime of the Ancient Mariner* (1798)
4 Rudyard Kipling, *Tomlinson* (1891)
5 Romans 12:15

a personality which, even if we would, we cannot unveil to human eyes. There are feelings sacred to the man who feels. We have to "dree our own weird,"[6] and live our own life, and die our own death.

In the time of desolation, when the truth of this solitude is borne in on us, we are left to ourselves, not because our friends are unfeeling, but simply because they are unable. It is not their selfishness which keeps them off, but just their frailty. Their spirit may be willing, but the flesh is weak. It is the lesson of life, that there is no stay in the arm of flesh, that even if there is no limit to human love, there is a limit to human power. Sooner or later, somewhere or other, it is the experience of every son of man, as it was the experience of the Son of Man, "Behold the hour cometh, and now is come, that ye my friends shall be scattered every man to his own, and shall leave me alone."[7]

Human friendship must have limits, just because it is human. It is subject to loss, and is often to some extent the sport of occasion. It lacks permanence; misunderstandings can estrange us; slander can embitter us; death can bereave us. We are left very much the victims of circumstances; for like everything earthly it is open to change and decay. No matter how close and spiritual the intercourse, it is not permanent, and never certain. If nothing else, the shadow of death is always on it. Tennyson describes how he dreamed that he and his friend should pass through the world together, loving and trusting each other, and together pass out into the silence.

Arrive at last the blessed goal,
And He that died in Holy Land
Would reach us out the shining hand,
And take us as a single soul.[8]

It was a dream at the best. Neither to live together nor to die to-

---

6 Scottish idiom meaning to face one's fate.

7 John 16:32

8 Alfred, Lord Tennyson, *In Memoriam* (1850)

gether could blot out the spiritual limits of friendship. Even in the closest of human relations, when two take each other for better for worse, for richer for poorer, in sickness and in health, they may be made one flesh, but never one soul. Singleness is the ultimate fact of human life. "The race is run by one and one, and never by two and two."[9]

In religion, in the deepest things of the spirit, these limits we have been considering are perhaps felt most of all. With even a friend who is as one's own soul, we cannot seek to make a spiritual impression, without realizing the constraint of his separate individuality. We cannot break through the barriers of another's distinct existence. If we have ever sought to lead to a higher life another whom we love, we must have been made to feel that it does not all rest with us, that he is a free moral being, and that only by voluntarily yielding his heart and will and life to the King, can he enter the Kingdom. We are forced to respect his personality. We may watch and pray and speak, but we cannot save. There is almost a sort of spiritual indecency in unveiling the naked soul, in attempting to invade the personality of another life. There is sometimes a spiritual vivisection which some attempt in the name of religion, which is immoral. Only holier eyes than ours, only more reverent hands than ours, can deal with the spirit of a man. He is a separate individual, with all the rights of an individual. We may have many points of contact with him, the contact of mind on mind, and heart on heart; we may even have rights over him, the rights of love; but he can at will insulate his life from ours. Here also, as elsewhere when we go deep enough into life, it is God and the single human soul.

The lesson of all true living in every sphere is to learn our own limitations. It is the first lesson in art, to work within the essential limitations of the particular art. But in dealing with other lives it is perhaps the hardest of all lessons, to learn, and submit to, our limitations. It is the crowning grace of faith, when we are willing to submit, and to leave those we love in the hands of God, as we leave

---

9 Rudyard Kipling, *Tomlinson* (1891)

ourselves. Nowhere else is the limit of friendship so deeply cut as here in the things of the spirit.

No man can save his brother's soul,
  Nor pay his brother's debt. [10]

Human friendship has limits because of the real greatness of man. We are too big to be quite comprehended by another. There is always something in us left unexplained, and unexplored. We do not even know ourselves, much less can another hope to probe into the recesses of our being. Friendship has a limit, because of the infinite element in the soul. It is hard to kick against the pricks, but they are meant to drive us toward the true end of living. It is hard to be brought up by a limit along any line of life, but it is designed to send us to a deeper and richer development of our life. Man's limitation is God's occasion. Only God can fully satisfy the hungry heart of man.

---

10 Matthew Arnold, "Obermann Once More" in *The New Poems* (1867)

Love him, and keep him for thy Friend, who, when all go away,
will not forsake thee, nor suffer thee to perish at the last.
~ THOMAS À KEMPIS

… Hush, I pray you!
What if this friend happened to be—God!
~ ROBERT BROWNING, Fears and Scruples

Chapter 9

The Higher Friendship

L ife is an education in love. There are grades and steps in it, occasions of varying opportunity for the discipline of love. It comes to us at many points, trying us at different levels, that it may get entrance somehow, and so make our lives not altogether a failure. When we give up our selfishness and isolation, even in the most rudimentary degree, a beginning is made with us that is designed to carry us far, if we but follow the leading of our hearts. There is an ideal toward which all our experience points. If it were not so, life would be a hopeless enigma, and the world a meaningless farce. There must be a spiritual function intended, a design to build up strong and true moral character, to develop sweet and holy life, otherwise history is a despair, and experience a hopeless riddle. All truly great human life has been lived with a spiritual outlook, and on a high level. Men have felt instinctively that there is no justification for all the pain, and strife, and failure, and sorrow of the world, if these do not serve a higher purpose than mere existence. Even our tenderest relationships need some more authoritative warrant than is to be found in themselves, even in the joy and hope they bring. That joy cannot be meant as an empty lure to keep life on the earth.

And spiritual man has also discovered that the very breakdown of human ties leads out to a larger and more permanent love. It is sooner or later found that the most perfect love cannot utterly satisfy the heart of man. All our human intercourse, blessed and helpful as it may be, must be necessarily fragmentary and partial. A man must discover that there is an infinite in him, which only the infinite can match and supply. It is no disparagement of human friendship to admit this. It remains a blessed fact that it is possible to meet devotion, which makes us both humble and proud; humble at the sight of its noble sacrifice, proud with a glad pride at its wondrous beauty. Man is capable of the highest heights of love. But man can never take the place of God, and without God life is shorn of its glory and divested of its meaning.

So the human heart has ever craved for a relationship, deeper and more lasting than any possible among men, undisturbed by change, unmenaced by death, unbroken by fear, unclouded by doubt. The limitations and losses of earthly friendship are meant to drive us to the higher friendship. Life is an education in love, but the education is not complete till we learn the love of the eternal. Ordinary friendship has done its work when the limits of friendship are reached, when through the discipline of love we are led into a larger love, when a door is opened out to a higher life. The sickness of heart which is the lot of all, the loneliness which not even the voice of a friend can dispel, the grief which seems to stop the pulse of life itself, find their final meaning in this compulsion toward the divine. We are sometimes driven out not knowing whither we go, not knowing the purpose of it; only knowing through sheer necessity that here we have no abiding city, or home, or life, or love; and seeking a city, a home, a life, a love, that hath foundations.[1]

We have some training in the love of friends, as if only to prove to us that without love we cannot live. All our intimacies are but broken lights of the love of God. They are methods of preparation for the great communion. Insofar even that our earthly friendships are helps to life, it is because they are shot through with the spiritual, and they prepare us by their very deficiencies for something more permanent. There have been implanted in man an instinct, and a need, which make him discontented, till he find content in God. If at any time we are forced to cease from man, whose breath is in his nostrils, it is that we may reach out to the infinite Father, unchanging, the same yesterday, today, and forever.[2] This is the clamant,[3] imperious need of man.

The solitude of life in its ultimate issue is because we were made for a higher companionship. It is just in the innermost sanctuary, shut to every other visitant, that God meets us. We are driven to God by the needs of the heart. If the existence of God was due to a purely intellectual necessity; if we believed in him only because our reason gave warrant for the faith; it would not matter much whether he really is, and whether we really can know him. But when the instincts of our nature, and the necessities of the heart-life demand God, we are forced to believe. In moments of deep feeling, when all pretence is silenced, a man may be still able to question the *existence*

---

1 Hebrews 11:10
2 Hebrews 13:8
3 Or urgent.

of God, but he does not question his own *need* of God. Man, to remain man, must believe in the possibility of this relationship with the divine. There is a love which passeth the love of women, passeth the love of comrades, passeth all earthly love, the love of God to the weary, starved heart of man.

To believe in this great fact does not detract from human friendship, but really gives it worth and glory. It is because of this, that all love has a place in the life of man. All our worships, and friendships, and loves, come from God, and are but reflections of the divine tenderness. All that is beautiful, and lovely and pure, and of good repute,[4] finds its appropriate setting in God; for it was made by God. He made it for himself. He made man with instincts, and aspirations, and heart-hunger, and divine unrest, that he might give them *full satisfaction in himself*. He claims everything, but he gives everything. Our human relationships are sanctified and glorified by the spiritual union. He gives us back our kinships, and friendships, with a new light on them, an added tenderness, transfiguring our common ties and intimacies, flooding them with a supernal joy. We part from men to meet with God, that we may be able to meet men again on a higher platform. But the love of God is the end and design of all other loves. If the flowers and leaves fade, it is that the time of ripe fruit is at hand. If these adornments are taken from the tree of life, it is to make room for the supreme fruitage. Without the love of God all other love would be but deception, luring men on to the awful disillusionment. We were born for the love of God; if we do not find it, it were better for us if we had never been born. We may have tasted of all the joys the world can offer, have known success and the gains of success, been blessed with the sweetest friendships and the fiercest loves; but if we have not found this the chief end of life, we have missed our chance, and can only have at the last a desolated life.

But if through the joy or through the sorrow of life, through love or the want of it, through the gaining of friends or the loss of them,

---

4 Philippians 4:8

we have been led to dower our lives with the friendship of God, we are possessed of the incorruptible, and undefiled, and that passeth not away.[5] The man who has it has attained the secret cheaply, though it had to be purchased with his heart's blood, with the loss of his dream of blessedness. When the fabric of life crumbled to its native dust, and he rose out of its wreck, the vision of the eternal love came with the thrill of a great revelation. It was the entrance into the mystery, and the wonder of it awed him, and the joy of it inspired him, and he awakened to the fact that never again could he be *alone* to all eternity.[6]

Communion with God is the great fact of life. All our forms of worship, all our ceremonies and symbols of religion, find their meaning here. There is, it is true, an ethic of religion, certain moral teachings valuable for life; there are truths of religion to be laid hold of by the reason; there are the consolations of religion to comfort the heart; but the root of all religion is this mystical union, a communion with the Unseen, a friendship with God open to man. Religion is not an acceptance of a creed, or a burden of commandments, but a personal secret of the soul, to be attained each man for himself. It is the experience of the nearness of God, the mysterious contact with the divine, and the consciousness that we stand in a special *individual* relationship with him. The first state of exaltation, when the knowledge burst upon the soul, cannot, of course, last; but its effect remains in inward peace, and outward impulse toward nobler life.

Men of all ages have known this close relationship. The possibility of it is the glory of life: the fact of it is the romance of history, and the true reading of history. All devout men that have ever lived have lived in the light of this communion. All religious experience has had this in common, that somehow the soul is so possessed by God, that doubt of his existence ceases; and the task of life becomes to keep step with him, so that there may be correspondence between

---

5 1 Peter 1:4

6 Psalm 48:14

the outer and the inner conditions of life. Men have known this communion in such a degree that they have been called preeminently the Friends of God,[7] but something of the experience which underlies the term is true of the pious of all generations.

To us, in our place in history, communion with God comes through Jesus Christ. It is an ineffable mystery, but it is still a fact of experience. Only through Jesus do we know God, his interest in us, his desire for us, his purpose with us. He not only shows us in his own example the blessedness of a life in fellowship with the Father, but he makes it possible for us. United to Jesus, we know ourselves united to God. The power of Jesus is not limited to the historical impression made by his life. It entered the world as history; it lives in the world as spiritual fact today. Martin Luther's experience is the experience of all believers: "To me it is not simply an old story of an event that happened once; for it is a gift, a bestowing, that endures forever." We offer Christ the submission of our hearts, and the obedience of our lives; and he offers us his abiding presence. We take him as our Master; and he takes us as his friends. "I call you no longer servants," he said to his disciples, "but I have called you friends."[8] The servant knoweth not what his Master doeth, his only duty is to obey; a friend is admitted to confidence, and though he may do the same thing as a servant, he does not do it any longer unreasoningly, but, having been taken into counsel, he knows why he is doing it. This was Christ's method with his disciples, not to apportion to each his task, but to show them his great purpose for the world, and to ask for their service and devotion to carry it out.[9]

The distinction is not that a servant pleases his master, and a friend pleases himself. It is that our Lord takes us up into a relationship of love with himself, and we go out into life inspired with his Spirit to work his work. It begins with the self-surrender of love;

---

7 James 2:23
8 John 15:15
9 Matthew 28:19-20

and love, not fear nor favour, becomes the motive. To feel thus the touch of God on our lives changes the world. Its fruits are joy, and peace, and confidence that all the events of life are suffused, not only with meaning, but with a meaning of love. The higher friendship brings a satisfaction of the heart, and a joy commensurate to the love. Its reward is itself, the sweet, enthralling relationship, not any adventitious gain it promises, either in the present, or for the future. Even if there were no physical, or moral, rewards and punishments in the world, we would still love and serve Christ *for his own sake.* The soul that is bound by this personal attachment to Jesus has a life in the eternal, which transfigures the life in time with a great joy.

We can see at once that to be the friend of God will mean peace also. It has brought peace over the troubled lives of all his friends throughout the ages. Every man who enters into the covenant, knows the world to be a spiritual arena, in which the love of God manifests itself. He walks no longer on a sodden earth and under a grey sky; for he knows that, though all men misunderstand him, he is understood, and followed with loving sympathy, in heaven. It was this confidence in God as a real and near friend, which gave to Abraham's life such distinction, and the calm repose which made his character so impressive. Strong in the sense of God's friendship, he lived above the world, prodigal of present possessions, because sure of the future, waiting securely in the hope of the great salvation. He walked with God in sweet unaffected piety, and serene faith, letting his character ripen in the sunshine, and living out his life as unto God not unto men. To know the love of God does not mean the impoverishing of our lives, by robbing them of their other sweet relations. Rather, it means the enriching of these, by revealing their true beauty and purpose. Sometimes we are brought nearer God through our friends, if not through their influence or the joy of their love, then through the discipline which comes from their very limitations and from their loss. But oftener the experience has been that, through our union with the Friend of friends, we are led into richer and fuller intercourse with our fellows. The nearer we get to the centre of the circle, the nearer we get to each other. To be joined together in Christ is the only permanent union, deeper than the tie of blood, higher than the bond of kin, closer than the most sacred earthly relationship. Spiritual kinship is the great nexus to unite men. "Who are my brethren?" asked Jesus, and for answer pointed to his disciples, and added, "Whosoever shall do the will of my Father in heaven, the same is my mother and sister and brother."[10]

We ought to make more of our Christian friendships, the communion of the saints, the fellowship of believers. "They that feared God spake often one with another,"[11] said the prophet Malachi in one of the darkest hours of the church. What mutual comfort, and renewed hope, they would get from, and give to, each other! Faith can be increased, and love stimulated, and enthusiasm revived by intercourse. The supreme friendship with Christ therefore will not take from us any of our treasured intimacies, unless they are evil. It will increase the number of them, and the true force of them. It will link us on to all who love the same Lord in sincerity and truth. It will open our heart to the world of men that Jesus loved and gave his life to save.

This friendship with the Lord knows no fear of loss; neither life, nor death, nor things present, nor things to come can separate us.[12] It is joy and strength in the present, and it lights up the future with a great hope. We are not much concerned about speculations regarding the future; for we know that we are in the hands of our Lover. All that we care to assert of the future is, that Christ will in an ever fuller degree be the environment of all Christian souls, and the effect of that constant environment will fulfil the aspiration of the apostle, "We shall be like him, for we shall see him as he is."[13] Communion produces likeness. This even now is the test of our friendship with the

---

10 Matthew 12:48-50
11 Malachi 3:16
12 Romans 8:38-39
13 1 John 3:2

Lord. Are we assimilating his mind, his way of looking at things, his judgments, his Spirit? Is the Christ-conscience being developed in us? Have we an increasing interest in the things which interest him, an increasing love of the things that he loves, an increasing desire to serve the purposes he has at heart? "Ye are my friends, if ye do whatsoever I command you,"[14] is the test by which we can try ourselves.

Fellowship with him, being much in his company, thinking of him, seeking to please him, will produce likeness, and bring us together on more intimate terms. For, as love leads to the desire for fuller fellowship; so fellowship leads to a deeper love. Even if sometimes we almost doubt whether we are really in this blessed covenant of friendship, our policy is to go on loving him, serving him, striving to please him; and we will yet receive the assurance, which will bring peace; he will not disappoint us at the last. It is worth all the care and effort we can give, to have and to keep him for our friend who will be a lasting possession, whose life enters into the very fibre of our life, and whose love makes us certain of God.

We ought to use our faith in this friendship to bless our lives. To have an earthly friend, whom we trust and reverence, can be to us a source of strength, keeping us from evil, making us ashamed of evil. The dearer the friend and the more spiritual the friendship, the keener will be this feeling, and the more needful does it seem to keep the garments clean. It must reach its height of intensity and of moral effectiveness in the case of friendship with God. There can be no motive on earth so powerful. If we could only have such a friendship, we see at once what an influence it might have over our life. We can appreciate more than the joy, and peace, and comfort of it; we can feel the *power* of it. To know ourselves ever before a living, loving Presence, having a constant sense of Christ abiding in us, taking him with us into the marketplace, into our business and our pleasure, to have him as our familiar friend in joy and sorrow, in gain and loss, in success and failure, must, in accordance with all

---

14 John 15:14

psychological law, be a source of strength, lifting life to a higher level of thought, and feeling, and action. Supposing it were true and possible, it would naturally be the strongest force in the world, the most effective motive that could be devised: it would affect the whole moral outlook, and make some things easy now deemed impossible, and make some things impossible now to our shame too easy. Supposing this covenant with God were true, and we knew ourselves to have such a Lover of our soul, it would, as a matter of course, give us deeper and more serious views of human life, and yet take away from us the burden and the unrest of life.

Unless history be a lie, and experience a delusion, it *is* true. The world is vocal with a chorus of witness to the truth of it. From all sorts and conditions of men comes the testimony to its reality—from the old, who look forward to this Friend to make their bed in dying; from the young, who know his aid in the fiery furnace of temptation; from the strong, in the burden of the day and the dust of the battle, who know the rest of his love even in the sore labour; from the weak, who are mastered by his gracious pity, and inspired by his power to suffer and to bear. Christ's work on earth was to make the friendship of God possible to all. It seems too good to be true, too wondrous a condescension on his part, but its reality has been tested, and attested, by generations of believers. This covenant of friendship is open to us, to be ours in life, and in death, and past the gates of death.

The human means of communication is prayer, though we limit it sadly. Prayer is not an act of worship merely, the bending of the knee on set occasions, and offering petitions in need. It is an attitude of soul, opening the life on the Godward side, and keeping free communication with the world of spirit. And so, it is possible to pray always,[15] and to keep our friendship ever green and sweet; and God comes back upon the life, as dew upon the thirsty ground. There is an interchange of feeling, a responsiveness of love, a thrill of mutual friendship:

---

15 1 Thessalonians 5:17

You must love him, ere to you
He will seem worthy of your love.[16]

The great appeal of the Christian faith is to Christian experience. Loving Christ is its justification as every loving heart knows. Life evidences itself: the existence of light is its own proof. The power of Christ on the heart needs no other argument than itself. Men only doubt when the life has died out, and the light has waned, and flickered, and spent itself. It is when there is no sign of the spirit in our midst, no token of forces beyond the normal and the usual, that we can deny the spirit. It is when faith is not in evidence that we can dispute faith. It is when love is dead that we can question love. The Christian faith is not a creed, but a life; not a proposition, but a passion. Love is its own witness to the soul that loves: communion is its own attestation to the spirit that lives in the fellowship. The man who lives with Jesus knows him to be a Lover that cleaves closer than a brother, a Friend that loveth at all times, and a Brother born for adversity.[17]

It does not follow that there is an end of the question, so far as we are concerned, if we say that we at least do not know that friendship, and cannot love him. Some even say it with a wistful longing, "Oh, that I knew where I might find him."[18] It is true that love cannot be forced, that it cannot be made to order, that we cannot love because we ought, or even because we want. But we can bring ourselves into the presence of the lovable. We can enter into friendship through the door of discipleship; we can learn love through service; and the day will come to us also when the Master's word will be true, "I call you no longer servant, but I call you friend."[19] His love will take possession of us, till all else seems as hatred in comparison.

---

16 William Wordsworth, *A Poet's Epitaph* (1799)

17 Proverbs 17:17; 18:24

18 Job 23:3

19 John 15:15

"All lovers blush when ye stand beside Christ," says Samuel Rutherford; "woe unto all love but the love of Christ. Shame for evermore be upon all glory but the glory of Christ; hunger for evermore be upon all heaven but Christ. I cry death, death be upon all manner of life but the life of Christ."

To be called *friends* by our Master, to know him as the Lover of our souls, to give him entrance to our hearts, is to learn the meaning of living, and to experience the ecstasy of living. The higher friendship is bestowed without money and without price,[20] and is open to every heart responsive to God's great love.

> *'Tis heaven alone that is given away,*
> *'Tis only God may be had for the asking.*[21]

---

20 Isaiah 55:1
21 James Russell Lowell, *The Birch-Tree* (1885)

Nothing is more refreshing to the soul (except communication with God himself) than the company and society of a friend.
~ ESTHER EDWARDS BURR

Friendship is the greatest of worldly goods. Certainly to me it is the chief happiness of life. If I had to give a piece of advice to a young man about a place to live, I think I should say, "Sacrifice almost everything to live where you can be near your friends."
~ C.S. LEWIS

Suggested Reading

Andrew Bonar, *The Life of Robert Murray M'Cheyne* (Edinburgh: The Banner of Truth Trust, 1978). [ISBN 978-0-851510-85-9].

Jonathan Edwards, *Charity and Its Fruits* (Edinburgh: The Banner of Trust Trust, 1991). [ISBN 978-0-851513-51-5].

Gary Inrig, *Quality Friendship* (Chicago: Moody Press, 1981). [ISBN 0-8024-2891-6].

C.S. Lewis, *The Four Loves* (New York: Harvest Books, 1991). [ISBN 978-0-15632-930-9].

Paul David Tripp, *Instruments in the Redeemer's Hands* (Phillipsburg, NJ: P&R Publishing, 2002). [ISBN 978-0-87552-607-2].

*Other titles available
from Joshua Press*

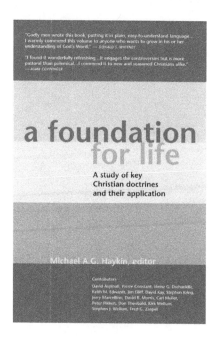

a foundation for life

A study of key
Christian doctrines
and their application

Michael A.G. Haykin, editor

Contributors:
David Aspinall, Pierre Constant, Heinz G. Dschankilic, Keith M. Edwards, Jim Elliff, David Kay, Stephen Kring, Jerry Marcellino, David B. Morris, Carl Muller, Peter Pikkert, Don Theobald, Kirk Wellum, Stephen J. Wellum, Fred G. Zaspel

A foundation for life

A study of key Christian doctrines and their application

Edited by Michael A. G. Haykin

ARE YOU TRYING to understand what the Christian faith is all about? Does studying Christian doctrine seem impractical to your daily life? Do you find some biblical teachings confusing? When things happen in your life do you find yourself questioning God's character? Are you confused about judgment? sanctification? sin? With these and many other questions in our minds, we have brought together some contemporary pastors and church leaders to help explain the basic doctrines of the Christian faith in an easy, understandable way. The impact of these truths should transform your life and help to renew our society.

JOSHUA PRESS / ISBN 1-894400-17-8

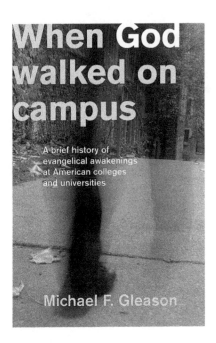

When God walked on campus

A brief history of evangelical awakenings at American colleges and universities

By Michael F. Gleason

HERE ARE SOME accounts of revivals in the past two centuries that will whet your appetite for the transforming work of God's Spirit on campuses today. From the halls of Princeton, Yale, Harvard, Dartmouth, Bethel, Wheaton, Trinity, Ashland, and many others, comes stories of awakening and revival. On both secular and Christian campuses, the moving of God was evident as men and women were converted and stirred to ministry and foreign service. Out of these awakenings came the formation of many of the student and campus fellowships still at work today.

JOSHUA PRESS / ISBN 1-894400-16-X

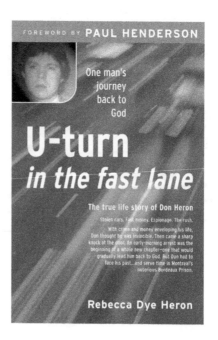

U-turn in the fast lane
One man's journey back to God

Foreword by Paul Henderson
By Rebecca Dye Heron

DON HERON KNEW about God as a child, but now he is trying to drive all that from his mind—he doesn't need God or the crutch of religion. From industrial espionage to the rush of crime, Don's every move seems to distance himself from God. When the swirl of auto theft, easy money, drinking and strip bars comes to a halt with his arrest, Don begins to face the hole he is in and look for the hope he will need to recover his misspent life— and he comes to know the power of God's forgiveness and the joy of a changed life! Don's life in the fast lane is transformed by a radical u-turn in his thinking.

JOSHUA PRESS / ISBN 1-894400-18-6

Fierce the conflict

By Norman H. Cliff

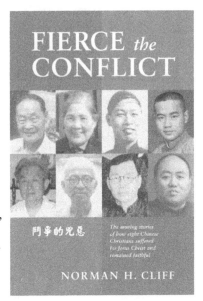

FIERCE THE CONFLICT relates the hardship and struggle of eight believers whose faith was tested through periods of persecution, imprisonment and forced labour in the difficult days of the "Accusation Meetings" and the traumatic ten years of China's Cultural Revolution.

ISBN 1-894400-12-7

Fresh springs
Essays by Tom Wells

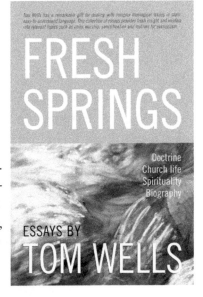

TOM WELLS' unusual ability to articulate complex theological issues into layman's terms has made his writings of immense value to the Christian church. These essays provides fresh insight and wisdom into relevant topics such as unity, worship, sanctification and motives for evangelism.

ISBN 1-894400-14-3

Deo Optimo et Maximo Gloria
To God, best and greatest, be glory

www.joshuapress.com